Visitors' Scotland

Visitors' Scotland

Jan Read
Maite Manjón

Acknowledgements
The authors wish to thank the Scottish Tourist Board and its Chief Executive, Philippe Taylor, for generous help in the research and preparation of the book and for providing many photographs. The Board's Publications Editor, John Hutchinson, and Senior Advisor to the Tourist Industry Advisory Service, R. Morrison-Smith, were of great assistance in checking the text. Our thanks also go to the National Trust for Scotland and Philip Sked for making available photographs from its library; to the Royal and Ancient Golf Club for permission to photograph in the club house; and to the library of the University of St. Andrews for leave to reproduce historical engravings and photographs from its collections.

First published 1979 by
Macmillan London Limited
London and Basingstoke

Associated companies in Delhi, Dublin,
Hong Kong, Johannesburg, Lagos, Melbourne,
New York, Singapore and Tokyo

Design by Hayes/Sterling Design Associates

Regional maps by R & B Art

Filmset by Filmtype Services Ltd., Scarborough
Printed in Hong Kong

British Library Cataloguing in Publication Data
Read, Jan
   Visitors' Scotland
   1. Scotland – Description and travel – 1951 –
   – Guide-books
   I. Title
   914.11'04'857   DA870

ISBN 0–333–24661–6

CONTENTS

Publications of the Scottish Tourist Board

Where to Stay in Scotland (in two parts: *Hotels and Guest Houses* and
    Bed and Breakfast)
Scotland: New Touring Map
Scotland for the Motorist
Camping and Caravan Sites in Scotland
Self Catering Accommodation in Scotland
Scotland: 600 Things to See
Scotland: In Famous Footsteps
Scotland for Children (Books 1 and 2)
Scotland Home of Golf
Angler's Guide to Scottish Waters
Walks and Trails in Scotland
Scotland for Hillwalking

Historic Hotels and Inns in Scotland
Farmhouse Accommodation
Tourist Information Centres
A Taste of Scotland
Scottish Castles, Country Houses & Mansions
See Scotland at Work
Events in Scotland: January–December
Scottish Entertainments
Boat and Yacht Charter
Adventure and Special Interest Holidays in Scotland
Pony Trekking and Riding Centres

These very helpful and practical publications may be obtained from local Tourist Information Centres, good bookshops, or direct from the Scottish Tourist Board, 23 Ravelston Terrace, Edinburgh EH4 3EU. A modest charge is made for those of the first group; the others are available free.

    The London address of the Scottish Tourist Board is 5 Pall Mall East, SWIY 5BA.

INTRODUCTION

Before embarking on the famous 'Tour of the Hebrides' with Dr. Johnson, Boswell mentioned their project to Voltaire. 'He looked at me, as if I had talked of going to the North Pole, and said, "You do not insist on my accompanying you?" — "No, sir" — "Then I am very willing you should go." ' And so the Doctor, relinquishing the 'felicity of a London life', set off with his companion in search of 'simplicity and wildness'.

Beautiful scenery and a sense of release from the pressures of everyday life are among the great pleasures of a holiday in Scotland, but there are many others. When Boswell attempted to expatiate on the beauties of the Firth of Forth, Johnson promptly pulled him up with, 'Ay, that is the state of the world. Water is the same everywhere'; and Johnson was at least as interested in character, conversation and the pleasures of the table as in the surroundings of mountain, loch and sea.

First and foremost Scotland is a country for people who like the open air — whether for the scenery or active participation in outdoor pursuits. On the subject of the water, Johnson was less than just. The essence of much of the loveliest Scottish landscape is the changing appearance of water: white and apparently motionless in the torrent descending from a distant hillside; peat-black in the pools of a river or cascading among its rocks and boulders; a mirror to the sky in a mountain-enfolded loch; or thrown back in sheets of spray against a cliff-bound coast. And where best to go for scenery? We suggest that you do not miss the mountainous coastline of Wester Ross; the crofting Hebrides; the almost treeless Orkneys and Shetlands, peopled by the ghosts of prehistory; the ominous defile of Glencoe; the luxuriant Trossachs; the smiling lochs of Perthshire or the mountain fastnesses of the Grampians and Cairngorms.

If you are a fisherman you will make for the great salmon and trout rivers — the Tweed in the Borders, the Tay, the Dee or the Spey in the North East — or one of the myriad lesser-known stretches of water. For sailors, there is the Caledonian Canal, or the yachting centres of the West, such as Oban and Tobermory. Rock climbers will want to pit their skills against the Cuillins in Skye or the cruel heights of Glencoe; while there are less exacting hill walks in the Central Highlands. Pony trekking in the forest parks of Argyll and Galloway is an energetic way of leaving the beaten track and also of exploring the wildlife reserves of the Cairngorms. In winter, too,

The Royal Arms of Scotland.

the snow-covered mountains are an attraction; and there are chair lifts for the ski slopes in Glenshee, the Cairngorms and Glencoe.

Golf is a national pastime – and not, as in foreign parts, a pursuit for the well-heeled and an excuse for clinching a business deal. There are more than 400 golf courses up and down Scotland, ranging from sporting Highland courses to the famous championship links at St. Andrews, Gleneagles, Turnberry, Muirfield and Carnoustie.

Whether you are interested in sports or sight-seeing, other attractions are the spring and summer festivals and Highland Gatherings. Of these, the most spectacular are the autumn International Festival in Edinburgh, with its concerts, plays, films and Military Tattoo, and the Royal Braemar Gathering, most celebrated of the Games, with competitions for tossing the caber, throwing the hammer and Highland reels. During the summer, the Pitlochry Festival Theatre is a centre for drama.

The most lasting reward of any visit to an unfamiliar country is to come away with a deepened knowledge of its people and traditions; and this in turn involves some understanding of its history. In Scotland, the physical remains are thick on the ground.

You might start in Orkney, visiting the great monoliths, the Stone Age village of Skara Brae and the Iron Age brochs or towers. In Argyll there are vestiges of the Scotti, who came from Ireland in the sixth century and gave Scotland its name, and whose missionaries built a monastery on Iona and spread Christianity throughout the country. Stirling Castle on its rocky crag and the battleground of Bannockburn nearby typify the Wars of Independence with England in the Middle Ages, while the places which most evoke the Reformation and the religious struggles of the sixteenth century are Edinburgh, with its castle, Royal Mile and the Palace of Holyrood House, and St. Andrews, for long the ecclesiastical capital of Scotland and the home of its oldest university. Culloden Moor, near Inverness, will always be remembered for Bonnie Prince Charlie's last and forlorn attempt to reinstate the dynasty of the Stuarts; and the ruined crofts of the Highlands and Islands stand as vivid testimony to the Clearances and mass emigration of the eighteenth and nineteenth centuries.

Some names keep recurring in the regional sections which follow. Most famous of the Dalriadic kings from Ireland was the doughty Kenneth MacAlpin, who by defeating the rival Picts in A.D. 843 united northern Scotland. There remained two other peoples, the Britons and the Angles, in the south of the country; and it was the achievement of Malcolm III, King of Scotland, called Canmore (1057–93), to bring effective government to the Lowlands as a whole (i.e. the part of the country lying south and east of the Highland Line, following the Forth and the Clyde and bounding the coastal areas of the North East). Malcolm spent part of his life as an exile in England, marrying the saintly Princess Margaret, granddaughter of Edmund Ironside, and became strongly imbued with Anglo-Norman ideas of feudalism, while his wife did much to temper the rough manners of the court and to introduce Roman Catholicism to Scotland.

The most outstanding of the freedom fighters in the war with England, which began with Edward I's attempt to reduce Scotland to vassalage and lasted for almost three centuries until the time of

Prince Charles Edward ('Bonnie Prince Charlie'), the Young Pretender, a painting by Antonio David.

Mary Queen of Scots, were William Wallace and Robert the Bruce. Wallace took arms against the invaders in 1297 and after a resounding victory at Stirling Bridge marched into England, but was defeated by Edward I at Falkirk the following year and exiled. When he later returned to wage guerrilla war he was outlawed, betrayed and executed in 1305 in London, where his head was placed on a pole on London Bridge as a warning to other 'traitors'.

Bruce, who first served under Wallace, is Scotland's national hero. During his early career he had to contend not only with the forces of Edward I, but with the supporters of his Scots rival the 'Red Comyn', whom he stabbed to death in a church in Dumfries. Although he was crowned king two months later in 1306, he spent the next year on the run in the Highlands. The turning point came with his defeat of the English at the Battle of Loudon Hill in 1307 and the death of Edward I shortly afterwards. Many of the great castles now fell into his hands, the most spectacular capture being that of Edinburgh, taken by his nephew, Sir Thomas Randolf, who scaled the face of the rock by night with thirty followers and overpowered the English garrison. Bruce assured the freedom of Scotland by his crushing defeat of the English at Bannockburn in 1314. He died of leprosy, contracted during his campaigns, in 1329.

Of all the rulers of Scotland the most haunting figure is that of Mary Queen of Scots. 'This was she', as Garrett Mattingly wrote, 'for whom Rizzio had died; and Darnley, the young fool; and Huntly, and Norfolk, and Babington and a thousand nameless men on the moors and gallows of the north. This was she whose legend had hung over England like a sword ever since she had galloped across its borders with her subjects in pursuit. This was the last captive princess of romance, the Dowager Queen of France, the exiled Queen of Scotland, the heir to the English throne . . .'

John Knox, from the second (French) edition of Theodore Beza's Vrais Portraits des Hommes Illustres, *1581. Unlike the portrait of Knox usually reproduced, this is authentic.*

Mary's real tragedy lay not in the murder of her luckless Italian favourite, her ill-judged marriage to her cousin, Darnley, or her subsequent and equally unsuitable marriage to the ruthless Bothwell, but in the fact that she was contending with the tide of history – a struggle from which few emerged unscathed. The daughter of James V of Scotland by a French Catholic mother, Mary of Guise and Lorraine, she was a queen before she was a week old and was subsequently to be at the mercy of rival factions jockeying for power. Brought up in France as a devout Catholic, she was married at the age of sixteen to the sickly Dauphin, later King Francis II of France. Eight months after his death she returned to Scotland in 1561 to find the country in the grip of the formidable and fanatic John Knox and pledged to a Calvanistic form of Protestantism. Although she did not attempt to halt the progress of the Reformed Church, only stipulating that she should be allowed to continue privately in her own faith, her sympathies were only too plain; and

Mary Queen of Scots as Dauphiness of France at the age of sixteen, a drawing by Clouet.

with Reformation sweeping Europe and in face of the corruption of the Roman Church in Scotland, the ultimate triumph of the Protestants was inevitable. The unpopularity of Mary's marriage to Bothwell forced her abdication in 1568 and her final flight to England. Her son by Darnley, James VI of Scotland and I of England, was to unite the crowns of the two countries in 1603.

Mary's death on the scaffold nineteen years after her escape to England perhaps obscures the fact that, more important than her tragic fate, the emergence of Calvinism in sixteenth-century Scotland was a turning point in the country's history. John Knox, no strict Puritan himself, could nevertheless note that 'The preachers were wondrous vehement in repression of all manner of vice . . . and especially avarice, oppression of the poor, excess, riotous cheer, banqueting, immoderate dancing, and whoredom, that thereof ensues'. It was not long before holidays such as Christmas, with its traditional carol singing, came under attack, whilst travel, recreation and drinking on Sundays were forbidden under pain of public repentance in church. All this has left a permanent mark on the Scottish character, although, to their credit, the Protestants were also responsible for inculcating a lasting respect for education, social justice and hard work, still so typical of the Scottish middle classes.

Jacobite sentiment lingered on, particularly in the Highlands, after the Treaty of Union in 1707, which combined the Parliaments of England and Scotland, and the accession of the first of the Hanoverians, George I. The last representative of the House of Stuart, Bonnie Prince Charlie, the Young Pretender, was also one of the most romantic. Handsome and swashbuckling, he sailed from France with only seven companions to raise his standard at Glenfinnan in August 1745 and lead his Highlanders deep into the heart of England. But local enthusiasm was not enough; he was compelled to retreat to Inverness and finally brought to book by the grimly professional Duke of Cumberland at Culloden. From then he was a hunted man and, after hiding for months in the mountains, he escaped to the Hebrides and later, with the help of the courageous Flora Macdonald, to France, where he died a penniless exile.

* * *

For administrative purposes Scotland is now divided into nine Regions and three Islands Authorities. These are: Highland, Grampian, Tayside, Fife, Lothian, Borders, Central, Strathclyde, Dumfries and Galloway, and the Islands Authorities of Orkney, Shetland and Western Isles. The areas described in the book cover the ground rather differently; they are listed in the Contents and illustrated in the sketch maps at the head of the following eight sections.

There are international airports at Prestwick, Glasgow, Edinburgh and Aberdeen, to which one may also fly from England; internal air services cover the main cities and many of the islands, including Orkney and Shetland. The populated areas are well served by rail, but north of Inverness the only routes are to Wick and Thurso and the picturesque West Highland line, winding by loch and mountainside, to Kyle of Lochalsh. Another scenic railway is that from Glasgow to Mallaig. It is also possible to see a great deal by using local buses or, in the more remote areas, the post buses, which carry a few passengers. The Highlands and Islands Development Board issues advantageous Travelpass tickets allowing unlimited travel by rail, bus and ferry in the Highlands and Islands, but perhaps the most comfortable and convenient way to see the country is by car. All of the larger islands are served by car ferries; and the principal companies, Caledonian MacBrayne Ltd. and Western Ferries Ltd., serving the Clyde ports and Western Islands, and P. & O. Ferries, sailing to Orkney and Shetland, operate some ships with cabins and organize very enjoyable short cruises during the summer season.

Many of the roads in the Highlands have been widened and straightened, but in the far North West and Islands there are still long stretches of narrow single-track road following the old cattle paths and twisting up and down hill through the heather, with passing places at intervals. Since they are sometimes bordered by deep ditches, the rule of the road is to drive slowly, keeping a look out for wandering sheep, and to pull in at the nearest passing place on the approach of a car in the opposite direction. Filling stations are sometimes few and far between in these parts, so keep your tank topped up.

A good touring map is a necessity; and one of the best is the 5 miles to 1 inch sheet published by the Scottish Tourist Board, which marks castles, gardens, nature reserves, information centres, youth hostels and other objects of interest.

On the subject of the Scottish weather, a witty Englishman, Sidney Smith, once wrote of the Scots: 'Their temper stands everything except an attack on their climate. They would have you believe they can ripen fruit; and, to be candid, I must own that in remarkably warm summers I have tasted peaches that make excellent pickles ... no nation has so large a stock of benevolence of heart.' Despite long-standing myths, Scotland is in fact no wetter than England: rainfall over the British Isles as a whole varies from east to west and not from north to south. Although wetter than the east, the west is milder and free from the cold winds of northern Europe; in sheltered sites palm trees and subtropical plants are a familiar sight. When visiting Scotland you may well bask in sunshine, but it is a sensible precaution to bring warm

The thirteenth-century Brig o' Doon at Alloway, mentioned in Burns's Tam o' Shanter.

sweaters. During the summer the daylight lasts much longer than in England or southern Europe. A round of golf is perfectly feasible after dinner, and in the far north the sky remains a pearly grey during the brief interval between sunset and sunrise.

Accommodation ranges from five star hotels, such as those at Gleneagles and Turnberry operated by British Transport Hotels and the converted castles and mansions offering luxury and country house surroundings, to medium-priced hotels, country inns and bed and breakfast places. In the medium price range the best value is often to be had at the traditional fishing hotels, but during the high season (July and August) these, like other hotels in the Highlands and holiday resorts, are very popular, so that reservations should be made well ahead. If you wish to tour as the spirit takes you and to stop on impulse, plan the visit for the late spring or autumn – both times to see the country at its best.

Many houses along the roadside, especially in the Highlands, hang out notices advertising bed and breakfast, and these are by no means to be ignored. The welcome is warm in every sense – in colder weather your hostess will light a fire in the sitting room – and, as Dr Johnson remarked: 'In the breakfast, the Scots, whether of the lowlands or mountains, must be confessed to excel us. The tea and coffee are accompanied not only with butter, but with honey, conserves, and marmalades [and, it may be added, with porridge, bacon and eggs, or kippers]. If an epicure could remove by a wish, in quest of sensual gratification, wherever he had supped he would breakfast in Scotland.'

Breakfast is always ample and good and, indeed, with a picnic lunch, will see you through to dinner. As regards other meals, times have changed since, as Marian McNeill wrote in *The Scots Kitchen*, 'Many a "lad o' pairts" who ultimately rose to fame studied his Bain and Aristotle by guttering candlelight in a garret in which one of the most conspicuous articles of furniture was a sack of oatmeal, and regular holidays were formerly granted by the authorities to enable the poor student to tramp back to his native glen and replenish his sack'. Scotland is, of course, famous for its game, salmon, trout and smoked fish, and there is a variety of good regional dishes, many of them described in the chapters which follow. The pity is that so many hotels serve 'international food' to visitors who would much prefer to try the local fare. Establishments serving at least a few traditional dishes are listed in the Scottish Tourist Board's *A Taste of Scotland* brochure and may be recognized by the 'Stockpot' sign at the door; other useful publications are its extremely comprehensive gazeteers, *Where to Stay in Scotland* (*Hotels and Guest Houses* and *Bed and Breakfast*).

The famous Scots high tea, in which a cooked dish is accompanied by an assortment of scones, bannocks and cakes, is no longer as universally popular as it once was, and most hotels now serve dinner. But the bakers' shops, with their pervading aroma of spice, hot sugar and yeast, flourish in every Scots town; and their fresh crusty bread, meat-filled bridies, mutton pies and enticing variety of cakes are the makings of a picnic.

Because of the ties with France, the Scots continued to drink claret when the English took to port — the liveliness of Scottish literature during the eighteenth century has sometimes been put down to the difference in drinking habits. Nowadays the wine lists, except in the more expensive hotels, are usually dull; but for people with a taste for malt whisky the choice and range of flavours is remarkable, especially in the Highlands (see Chapter 5). Scots licensing hours — a legacy of the Presbyterian tradition — have long been a puzzle to visitors. Until recently public houses were not open on Sundays, while at bars in the hotels sabbath day drinking was (and is) limited to 12.30 p.m. to 2.30 p.m. and 6.30 p.m. to 11 p.m. Residents in hotels, on the other hand, are entitled to order drinks for themselves and their guests at any time. The position has just changed, and Sunday opening of public houses is now permitted during the prescribed hours. Not all of them have taken advantage of this relaxation, and especially in the North West and the Islands, where the influence of the strictly Calvinistic 'Wee Frees' is strongest, many remain firmly closed. Not so very many years ago visitors' cars were locked in the garage in this area on Sundays, and light literature was removed and replaced by the Bible.

Until after the Second World War it was business as usual on Christmas Day throughout the country, and the winter holiday was celebrated at the New Year. The Scots now make the best of both worlds; but, except by the banks, English Bank Holidays are not observed in Scotland, each town or district fixing its own public holidays.

Although the coinage is the same, all the Scottish banks issue their own paper money, and since a note with a view of the Forth Bridge or a portrait of Robert Burns is not always familiar in England, it is advisable to change them before crossing the Border.

For additional information the reader is referred to the extensive and very helpful publications of the Scottish Tourist Board, listed at the start of the book. Besides those already mentioned they include booklets on caravan and camping sites, accommodation in farms and historic houses, golf, fishing, pony trekking, sailing and other outdoor activities. Useful books, guides and maps are available from the Scottish Highlands and Islands Development Board, P.O. Box 7, Inverness IV1 1QR. The National Trust for Scotland and the Department of the Environment also publish a wide range of literature describing the many historic sites and gardens in their care.

THE SOUTH EAST

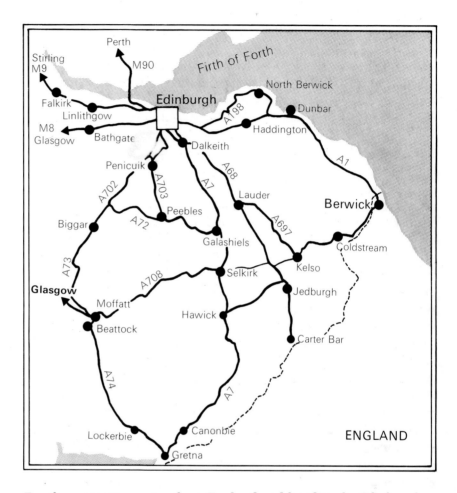

For the motorist coming from England and heading for Edinburgh, the South East is the first taste of Scotland. The region falls into two parts: the large area loosely known as the Borders, lying south of the Lammermuir, Moorfoot and Pentland hills, with rolling wooded country to the east and a miniature Highlands to the west; and the narrow, low-lying strip of Lothian sandwiched between the hills and the Firth of Forth, with Edinburgh at its centre.

All the main roads from England to the South East – the A1 through Berwick, the A697 by Coldstream, the A68 from just north of Scotch Corner and the A7 from Carlisle – pursue their different ways to Edinburgh. The A68, which follows the old Roman road into Scotland, is perhaps the most rewarding, although there are fine views of the cliffs and promontories of the southeast coast from the A1.

Beginning with a splendid panorama from the high pass of Carter Bar, where it enters Scotland, the A68 continues through Jedburgh and skirts Dryburgh, both with their ruined abbeys. If you then branch off on to the A72, it will take you to Melrose and Galashiels, through the Scott country and beautiful woods and hills to Peebles, and thence via the A703 to Edinburgh. Some of the most spectacular Border country lies to the west of this route along the A708 towards Moffat, which runs across the moorlands of Ettrick Forest, past St. Mary's Loch enfolded in barren heather-clad mountains, and near the Grey Mare's Tail, a waterfall descending all of 200 feet from Loch Skene through a cleft in the hills.

Although the South East was the first part of Scotland to benefit from the civilizing influence of the Angles, the Borders long remained one of the most turbulent and fought-over areas of the country thanks to the perpetual wars with England and the unruly character of its inhabitants, owing allegiance to the contentious families of Musgraves, Elliots, Kerrs, Hopes, Armstrongs and the rest.

The humanizing trend is exemplified by the four great Border abbeys of Dryburgh, Jedburgh, Kelso and Melrose, all founded during the reign of David I (1124–53). Apart from their Christianizing mission, the monks did much to foster sheep farming and agriculture in the region. The mellow ruins in red sandstone, set amongst green lawns and gravestones, bear mute testimony to the depredations of the Earl of Hertford in 1544–5 and the subsequent decline of the abbeys during the Reformation, when the few remaining brethren lost interest in all but their own material benefit.

Dirleton Castle, at the centre of one of the most picturesque villages in the South East.

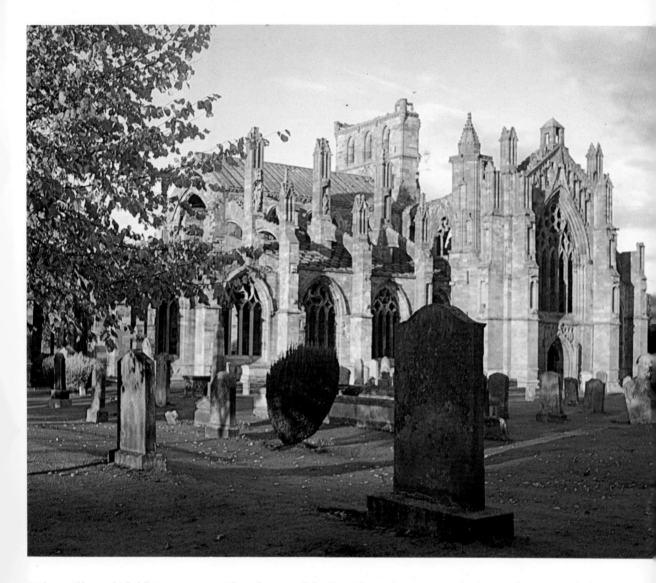

Melrose Abbey, which fell into ruins after the Reformation.

Hermitage Castle, a former stronghold of the Douglas family.

The shattered hulks of castles are so thick on the ground that only a few can be singled out. Hermitage, in Liddisdale near the Border, standing foursquare with the great arched entrance piercing its grim walls, was a seat of the Douglas family and the brief resting place of Mary Queen of Scots on her dash to meet Bothwell in 1566; Hume, on its hilltop near Kelso, dating from the thirteenth century, was largely destroyed by Cromwell in 1651, but was restored as an eighteenth-century folly; the massive ruins of Tantallon, another stronghold of the Douglases which also fell to Cromwell's army, surmount the cliffs near North Berwick against a breath-taking backdrop of sea and sky, with the Bass Rock gannetry close inshore; while the gaunt shell of Dirleton rises from a walled garden at the heart of a village almost English in character with its wide central green surrounded by yews.

17

Local fighting along the Border continued throughout the sixteenth century with the irruption of armed bands from both sides carrying off sheep and cattle, despite the appointment of Wardens of the Marches to keep the peace. In the words of one Scots reiver, as he passed a haystack, 'had ye but fower [four] feet ye shouldna stan' lang there'. A famous ballad recounts how James V tricked the redoubtable John Armstrong and his followers into surrender, thereupon hanging them on the spot; but it required firmer disciplinary action by his grandson James VI before the Borders were finally pacified.

With the advent of quieter times in the seventeenth century, the style of architecture changed, and castles gave way to houses designed for comfortable habitation. Among these pride of place must go to Traquair, off the A72 near Peebles, dating back to the tenth century and said to be the oldest continuously inhabited house in Scotland. No less than twenty-seven Scottish and English monarchs, including Mary Queen of Scots, have visited it. The tradition goes that the main gates with their flanking stone bears, now shut, were closed in 1746 after the fifth Earl had entertained the Young Pretender and promised that they should not be re-opened until the Stuarts were restored to the throne. The house contains a wealth of furniture, tapestries, books and historical relics; do not miss the eighteenth-century brewhouse, restored and operated by the present Laird for the production of the famous Traquair ale.

Left: Traquair House, reputedly the oldest continuously inhabited residence in Scotland.

Below: Holyrood Palace, Edinburgh, so closely associated with Mary Queen of Scots.

Other houses of particular interest near Kelso are the vast Floors Castle, said to number a window for every day of the year and built by William Adam in 1721; and Mellerstain House, also begun by William Adam and completed and decorated by his son, Robert, of whose work it is an outstanding example.

The Borders will always be associated with Sir Walter Scott, who did so much to arouse interest in his native country, and for many of whose historical novels Edinburgh and the Borders provide the setting. The story of his publisher's bankruptcy and of his heroic pledge that 'this right hand shall work it all off' is well known, as is that of his creation of Abbotsford House. Overlooking the Tweed near Melrose and planned as a treasure house of Scottish history, it was unkindly described by Ruskin as 'perhaps the most incongruous pile that gentlemanly modernism ever designed'. The interior, substantially unaltered since Scott's time, contains a fine collection of weapons, and relics such as Rob Roy's purse, broadsword and dirk; Bonnie Dundee's pistol; James VI's hunting bottle; and Prince Charles Edward's quaich (or drinking vessel). The human interest centres on Scott's study and his library of some 9000 volumes. Looking at the titles at random, it is easy to see where he drew the inspiration and historical detail for his novels; while the confined little study, with its gallery, spiral iron stair and the desk and chair at which he worked, conjure up the unremitting effort towards paying off the immense debt, which so told on his health and shortened his life.

Abbotsford House on the Tweed, planned by Sir Walter Scott as a treasure house of Scottish history.

Sir Walter Scott, from a painting by Andrew Geddes, A.R.A.

Festivals and Games

It seems that the Games, now
celebrated up and down the
Highlands, originated in Celtic times
and were first held in the presence
of the king and druids. They were
warlike in character, and
competitions were held to pick out
the strongest and fleetest men as
bodyguards and messengers. It is
said that Malcolm Canmore (see
page 8), who is credited with
founding the first Royal Braemar
Gathering, organized a hill race to
the summit of Craig Choinnich,
overlooking the place, to choose a

*Previous page: Edinburgh International
Festival, the military tattoo. Left: The
Lonach Gathering, march of the
clansmen. Right: Aviemore Highland
Games, a girl dancer. Below: The
Lonach Gathering, pipe major.*

Above: The Curlers, *by Sir George Harvey. Left: The Lonach Gathering, putting the shot.*

gille-ruith or running footman. In the past, the games always opened with a march of the clansmen, but this tradition survives only at the colourful Lonach Gathering, held in the little village of Strathdon in the mountains west of Aberdeen.

Above: Edinburgh International Festival, gymnasts on Calton Hill.
Left: Edinburgh International Festival, firework display.

After the Battle of Culloden and the Disarmament Act of 1747 (see page 91) the Gatherings fell into abeyance, but by the 1780s Highland societies were being formed to revive traditional music and dance, and a Gathering at Falkirk in 1781 led to the progressive restitution of the Gatherings as they are held today – the first taking place at St. Fillans in 1819. Other Gatherings were in the course of time to be celebrated at Crieff, Aboyne, Ballater and over the Highlands at large, the most famous being that at Braemar. It attracted the patronage of Queen Victoria and Prince Albert, and the

25

Left: Edinburgh International Festival, posters. *Below*: The Common an annual event in Galashiels.

Royal Braemar Gathering was for a time held in the grounds of Balmoral Castle.

At the heart of any Gathering are the 'heavy events', such as putting the stone, throwing the hammer, tossing the caber and wrestling. These made use of the primitive implements to be found in any agricultural community – the 'stones of strength', the blacksmith's hammer or the caber (*cabar* being the Gaelic for a tree trunk). The 'light events' include running and jumping, and competitions for piping and Highland dancing are another feature of the modern games.

The games held in Deeside and the North East are best known for athletic events, while the best piping is traditionally to be found in the Highlands and Islands of the west coast. Perhaps the most famous of all pipers are the fabled MacCrimmons, hereditary pipers to the Macleods of Dunvegan Castle, who founded their College of Piping nearby. The Gatherings most reputed for piping are the Northern Meeting held in Inverness and the Argyllshire Gathering at Oban.

The festivals celebrated in Scotland during the summer comprise a great deal more than those devoted to athletic contests, dancing and piping. There is the well-known Pitlochry Theatre Festival and, most famous of all, the Edinburgh International Festival. Inaugurated as a festival of the opera, concerts, chamber music and theatre by John Christie and Rudolf Bing in 1947 as a brave and colourful gesture amidst the austerity of post-war Britain, and lasting for three weeks towards the end of August and beginning of September, it attracts scores of thousands of visitors. For many, the highlight is the military tattoo with its massed pipe bands, held at night against the background of the floodlit castle.

The Borders are Scotland's horse country, and the tradition continues today with establishments for the breeding of horses, race meetings and the increasingly popular pony trekking. The Borders are also the original home of the hardy black-faced and Cheviot sheep, later introduced to the Highlands with such grim social repercussions; and towns such as Hawick, Galashiels and Selkirk have for long been the centre of a thriving weaving and knitwear industry. With a little notice, firms which are household names for their fine sweaters and cardigans, such as Peter Scott and Pringles in Hawick, will arrange tours of their mills for visitors — it is fascinating to see the numerous operations and the meticulous care that go to the making of a simple sweater — while Ballantynes at Walkerburn run the Scottish Museum of Wool Textiles in connection with their tweed manufactory. Here you may see yarn being spun on a primitive spindle or with the traditional spinning wheel.

Knitting the cuff of a sweater at Peter Scott Ltd. in Hawick, the first stage in manufacture.

Lothian cannot compare scenically with the Borders: its centre has been increasingly invaded by urban sprawl from Edinburgh, while West Lothian, with its slag heaps, motorways and the petrochemical complex at Grangemouth on the Firth of Forth, is one of Scotland's main industrial belts. Nevertheless, Dunbar and North Berwick on an unspoilt stretch of coast to the east are pleasant seaside resorts with good golf courses, and the dignified Royal Burgh of Haddington nearby has some fine streets dating from the eighteenth and nineteenth centuries. Lothian, like Edinburgh, is closely associated with Mary Queen of Scots. It was at Craigmillar Castle, on the southern outskirts of the city, that, with or without her connivance, the compact was signed for the murder of her husband, Darnley, 'sic ane young fool and proud tirrane'. Even in Mary's time the mediaeval castle had been much rebuilt after its devastation by the Earl of Hertford; it was one of her favourite residences, and a group of cottages once occupied by her attendants is still known as Little France.

To the west of Edinburgh along the Firth of Forth lies the splendid ruined palace of Linlithgow, begun by James I early in the fifteenth century, where Mary was born in 1542. It was burned,

probably by accident, during its occupation by government troops after the '45 rebellion. Nearer Edinburgh and within sight of the great rail and road bridges across the Forth is Hopetoun House. Set in 100 acres of parkland, frequented by red deer and rare four-horned St. Kilda sheep, it is the largest mansion in Scotland to be decorated by the Adam brothers and a magnificent example of their work. At Cramond, off the approach to the Forth road bridge, you may inspect the foundations of a Roman fort, one of the few surviving north of the Border.

Edinburgh is the Mecca of many visitors to Scotland, not least because of the International Festival held for three weeks at the end of August and beginning of September; and, more than the capital of Scotland, it is unquestionably one of the loveliest cities in Europe. Its historical and literary associations — with David Hume, Sir Walter Scott, R. L. Stevenson and others — are so extensive and there is so much of interest to see, that it would be out of place to attempt more than the briefest of descriptions.

The mediaeval axis of the city is the Royal Mile, running uphill from the Palace of Holyroodhouse, in the shadow of the towering Arthur's Seat, to the Castle on its volcanic crag at the far end. Both are inextricably and romantically linked with Mary, Queen of Scots: Holyrood because it was her residence for six years, the scene of her stormy meetings with John Knox, and the place where her Italian secretary, Rizzio, was brutally murdered in her presence; and the Castle because it was the birthplace of her son, James VI. Between these two focal points the narrow street with its over-hanging houses passes the much reconstructed St. Giles Cathedral, with the old Parliament Hall and old Quadrangle of Edinburgh University to its rear, John Knox's House and Huntly House, now the home of the City Museum.

The Forth rail bridge, with the modern road bridge in the background.

From the Castle there can be seen a magnificent panorama of Princes Street, running through the heart of modern Edinburgh, and beyond it, of the elegant terraces, squares and crescents of the New Town, planned in 1767 and completed during the early nineteenth century. Princes Street, flanked on one side by shops and restaurants and on the other by spacious gardens, the Scott Monument and the Scottish National Gallery, is unforgettable. At its eastern end, above Waverley Station and the neo-Gothic bulk of the North British Hotel, are the heights of Calton Hill, once described as 'the Acropolis of that purposeful new Athenian Edinburgh of the Regency', and the site of the projected Scottish Assembly. It was by the Calton Steps that D. O. Hill and Robert Adamson, pioneers and old masters of calotype photography, opened their studio in 1843.

'Man,' said Mr. Peregrine Touchwood, otherwise known as the Cleikum Nabob, in Scott's *St. Ronan's Well*, 'is a cooking animal.' Elaborating on his theme at the institution of the Cleikum Cooking Club in an old Border inn, he went on: 'I have been telling my friend that the Reformation has thrown back the science of cooking three centuries in this corner of the island. Popery and made dishes, eh, Mr. Cargill? — Episcopacy, roast beef, and plumpudding — and what is left to the Presbytery but its lang-kail, its brose, and mashlum bannocks? . . . There is not a bare-foot monk, sir, of the most beggarly abstemious order but can give you some pretty notions of tossing up a fricassee or an omelet, or of mixing an olio. Scotland has absolutely retrograded in gastronomy. Yet she saw a better day, the memory of which is savoury in our nostrils yet, Doctor. In old Jacobite families, and in the neighbourhood of decayed monasteries — in such houses as this, for instance, where long succeeding generations have followed the trade of victuallers — a few relics may still be found . . .'

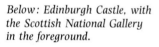

Below: Edinburgh Castle, with the Scottish National Gallery in the foreground.

The hostess of Scott's Cleikum Club was a Mistress Margaret Dods, and somewhat later, in 1826, a Mrs. Johnston of Edinburgh used the pseudonym when writing her *Cook and Housewife's Manual*, which began a renaissance of Scots cooking.

It is hardly surprising that Edinburgh, with its long French tradition, should have been the birthplace of so much that is best in the Scots cuisine. And today authentic Scots dishes may still be tasted at their best in restaurants such as Clarinda's and the Howtowdie. South east of Edinburgh, that most comfortable of hotels, the Open Arms at Dirleton, offers one of the most comprehensive Scots menus in the country.

LORRAINE SOUP

So named because it is said to have been introduced by Mary of Guise and Lorraine, mother of Mary Queen of Scots.

1 oz (30 g) butter
1 oz (30 g) cornflour
2 pints (12 dl) chicken stock
4 oz (120 g) chicken meat, finely chopped
Lemon zest, grated
Nutmeg, grated

Salt and pepper
4 tablespoons cream
1 oz (30 g) ground or flaked almonds
2 egg yolks, hard-boiled
Chopped parsley

Make a roux with the butter and cornflour and add it to the stock in a saucepan. Bring to the boil, add the chopped chicken, lemon zest, nutmeg, and salt and pepper to taste, then simmer for about 10 minutes. Now stir in the cream and flaked almonds. Pour into soup plates and garnish with the sieved egg yolks and chopped parsley.

Herriot's Hospital, Edinburgh, from Scotland Illustrated, *1853.*

A Border farm near Peebles.

MUSSEL AND ONION STEW

A traditional dish from the Edinburgh region; the recipe is from the Open Arms Hotel at Dirleton.

$2\frac{1}{2}$ lb (1 kg) mussels
2 oz (60 g) shallots, finely chopped
$\frac{1}{2}$ pint (3 dl) dry white wine
$1\frac{1}{2}$ pint (9 dl) fish stock
3 oz (80 g) butter
1 oz (30 g) flour
4 fl oz (12 ml) cream
Salt and pepper
Juice of $\frac{1}{2}$ lemon
Pinch of cayenne pepper

Thoroughly scrape and wash the mussels, then place them in a saucepan with the shallots, wine and fish stock. Cover and cook briskly for about 5 minutes until the shells open. Remove the mussels with a slotted spoon, place them on a plate and remove the beards and shells, then transfer them to a serving dish and keep warm.

Meanwhile strain the cooking liquid into a clean saucepan, reduce by half, and thicken it with a kneaded mixture of the flour and half of the butter. Blend in the cream and remaining butter, check the seasoning and add the lemon juice and a little cayenne pepper. Add the mussels and reheat, but do not boil, otherwise they will become tough.

TWEED KETTLE

A favourite nineteenth-century recipe from Edinburgh, which preserves the delicate flavour of the salmon.

2 lb (1 kg) fresh middle-cut salmon

Fish stock (sufficient to cover the salmon)

1 glass dry white wine

Salt and pepper

Ground mace

2 chopped shallots or 2 tablespoons chopped chives

1 tablespoon chopped parsley

2 oz (60 g) butter

2 oz (60 g) cornflour

Poach the salmon for 30 minutes in the fish stock and wine, seasoned with salt and pepper to taste and a little mace. Remove the fish, skin and bone it, and transfer to the hot serving dish to keep it warm. Reduce the liquid by two thirds, strain it and return to the pan. Now add the shallots or chives and the parsley, blend in the butter and cornflour, and adjust the seasoning. Stir the sauce well and pour it over the fish. Serve with boiled potatoes and garden peas.

STOVED HOWTOWDIE WI' DRAPPIT EGGS

A Scots way of braising or stewing chicken. 'Howtowdie' is a corruption of a French word meaning a young hen which has not laid, and the 'Drappit Eggs' refers to the method of dropping them into water to cook.

A little flour, seasoned with salt and pepper

4 breasts of chicken, or other jointed chicken

2 oz (60 g) butter

1½ lb (700 g) potatoes, peeled and sliced in rounds

½ lb (225 g) onions, peeled and sliced in rounds

½ pint (3 dl) chicken stock

Salt and pepper

½ lb (225 g) cooked spinach

4 poached eggs

Flour the pieces of chicken, brown them in a frying pan in butter, remove and reserve. Line the bottom of a casserole with a layer of potatoes and one of onions, put the pieces of chicken on top and add the stock. Top with a final layer of sliced potato and season with pepper and salt. Cover the casserole with a lid and cook for about 2 hours in a moderate oven (Mark 4, 350°F). Remove the lid 10 minutes before the cooking time is up and brush the potatoes with a little butter to brown the top.

Serve with cooked spinach, topped by a poached egg.

THE SOUTH WEST

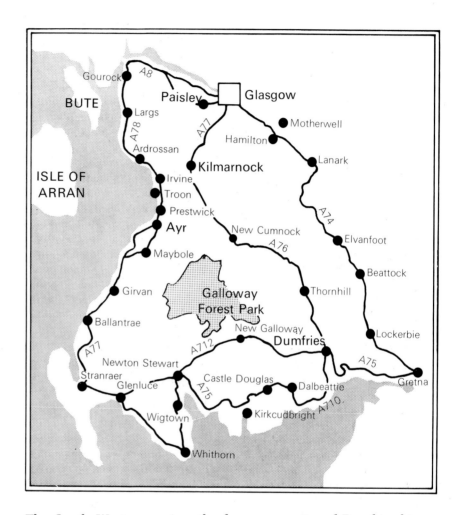

The South West comprises the former counties of Dumfriesshire, Kirkcudbrightshire, Wigtonshire, Ayrshire, Lanarkshire and Renfrewshire, together with Glasgow and the islands of Bute and Arran — broadly the area west of the A74 running from Carlisle to Glasgow. The Kintyre peninsula is more of a piece with Argyll and is described in Chapter 4.

With its wide expanses of moorland, numerous small lochs and mountains rising as high as the 2766-foot Merrick in the heart of the Galloway Forest Park, contrasting with well-wooded farmland and small, well-kept towns, this is one of the least known parts of Scotland and well worth a visit. Whether you start from Glasgow or Prestwick, to the north, or Gretna, on the Border, it is a question

of striking into the old kingdom of Galloway, roughly south of a line from Ayr, to see the region at its unspoilt best.

The picturesque little town of Kirkcudbright.

Some two centuries before St. Columba arrived in Iona, the native-born St. Ninian began preaching Christianity in the South West and founded the first church in Scotland at Whithorn, near Wigtown, in A.D. 397. The ruins of its Priory date from the twelfth century; and the subsequent progress of Christianity is marked by early memorial stones, such as the Latinus Stone at Whithorn, the Kirkmadrine Stones in the Rhinns of Galloway, the hammer-shaped peninsula at its south western tip, the cross at Ruthwell, near Dumfries, and the great abbeys, of which the most impressive, both ruined, are Dundrennan, near Kirkcudbright, and Sweetheart, south of Dumfries. It was at Dundrennan that Mary Queen of Scots, after her defeat at Langside, is said to have spent her last night in Scotland before her ill-fated flight to England; and Sweetheart is so named because its founder, Devorgilla Balliol, was buried there with the heart of her husband, which she had carried with her for some sixteen years.

Their son, King John Balliol, who surrendered so abjectly to Edward I, was the rival of Robert the Bruce; and the South West is closely linked with the Wars of Independence, since both Wallace and Bruce were born in the region and it was here that they began their struggles against the English. Towards the end of his life Bruce, then sick with leprosy, made a pilgrimage to Whithorn; the chapel of his lepers' hospital and the legendary Bruce's Well may still be seen at Prestwick.

Galloway was a stronghold of the Covenanters and the scene of many encounters with the rival Episcopalians during the seventeenth century. Especially between 1684 and 1688, the 'killing time', there were many Covenanting martyrs, commemorated by the stones and tombs with their poignant inscriptions scattered through the area. One such in Galloway Forest Park has carved upon it both the names of six Covenanter martyrs and of the men who murdered them.

This is also the Burns Country. Robert Burns, Scotland's finest poet, was hardly the unschooled ploughman of popular tradition,

Robert Burns, Scotland's premier poet.

and for all his lyrical poems rooted in the life of the Scottish countryside, he was perfectly capable of holding his own with Sir Walter Scott and the literary lions of Edinburgh. In view of the enormous interest in his life, The Scottish Tourist Board publishes a series of booklets and pamphlets, outlining a 'Burns Heritage Trail' embracing the various places in the South West with which he was most closely associated. The centre of the Burns cult is the village of Alloway on the outskirts of Ayr; here you may visit the cottage where he was born in 1759, a museum with an extensive collection of his personal belongings and manuscripts, the thirteenth-century Brig o' Doon immortalized in *Tam o' Shanter* and a modern exhibition centre, featuring a well-made audiovisual presentation of his life and times. Other places intimately connected with him are Kilmarnock, where the first edition of his poems was published in 1786, Ellisland Farm near Dumfries, where he unsuccessfully tried to introduce new methods of agriculture, and Dumfries itself, where he spent the last years of his life as an exciseman.

The scenic centre of the region is the Galloway Forest Park, covering some 150,000 acres of hills, forests and lochs – the largest, Loch Ken, tree-fringed with the charming little town of New Galloway at its head, lying somewhat to the east. The best way of exploring the area is on pony back.

The ruins of Sweetheart Abbey.

Culzean Castle near Turnberry, magnificently reconstructed and decorated by Robert Adam.

To the south east of the Forest lie the vast sands of the Solway Firth, so swiftly inundated by the treacherous tidal bore; while further west there is a string of attractive and unspoilt little towns, notably Castle Douglas, Kirkcudbright, Gatehouse of Fleet and Newton Stewart. Kirkcudbright, with its fishing quay, the ruins of an old castle and dignified eithteenth-century streets, is a favourite with painters and photographers. The climate in these parts is exceptionally mild, and gardens such as Threave near Castle Douglas and Logan in the Rhinns of Galloway abound in azaleas, rhododendrons, tree ferns, cabbage palms and other plants from temperate and semi-tropical areas.

Of the many castles testifying to the region's turbulent and feuding past, perhaps the two best worth a visit are Bothwell, nine miles south east of Glasgow, one of the finest thirteenth-century castles in the country, reconstructed by the Douglases in the fifteenth century, and Culzean on the coast near Turnberry. Culzean, standing on the cliffs at the edge of a magnificent park and nature reserve, belongs to the National Trust for Scotland, which has spent some £500,000 in renovating and furnishing it and in restoring the decorations to the original designs of Robert Adam. A mediaeval stronghold of the Kennedy family, it was entirely rebuilt by Robert Adam during 1777–92 and remains one of his most splendid achievements. Particularly noteworthy are the great oval staircase and the round drawing room, with its painted and moulded ceiling. A visitors' centre, housed in the old Home Farm, contains an imaginative exhibition illustrating the development of the estate and eighteenth-century agricultural improvements.

Turnberry nearby is famous for its golf courses, some of the best in Scotland; and there are other good courses at Ayr, Prestwick and Troon, bustling holiday playgrounds for Glasgow. The offshore islands of Arran and Bute are also favourites with summer visitors. Arran, with its mountains rising to 2800 feet, offers climbing and pony trekking as well as swimming, boating, fishing and golf; while the principal attraction on Bute is Rothesay, most popular of the resorts on the Clyde islands.

North of Troon the coastal area becomes increasingly industrialized, though there are pleasant stretches between Ardrossan and Gourock, beyond which shipbuilding and heavy industry take over in earnest in Greenock and Port Glasgow.

It was in Glasgow and the area to the south east that the Industrial Revolution first took root in Scotland in towns such as Kilmarnock, Lanark and Paisley. The union of Scotland with England in 1707 meant the removal of restrictions on Scottish trade with the colonies; and Glasgow soon became the most important tobacco port in Great Britain, exporting Scots manufactures in return, of which the most important was linen, first a product of cottage industry and later made in factories. After the American War of Independence in 1776—83 the colonists became free to sell their tobacco where they pleased. The trade disappeared overnight, and for the next fifty years Scottish industry was dominated by the manufacture of cotton textiles, especially in the mills of Renfrewshire and Lanarkshire, worked by water power.

Yet again disturbance in the United States disrupted industry in Scotland; and after the end of the Civil War and resumption of cotton exports, the cotton trade was very largely lost to Lancashire. The last phase was the development of the iron industry, dating from the opening of the Carron Works in Falkirk in 1760. Smelting, iron-founding and mining, and later steel-making, heavy engineering and shipbuilding were thereafter to remain the most important of Scotland's industries. During the nineteenth century almost every advance in marine engineering took place on Clydeside, which, despite subsequent recessions, has become synonymous with the building of ships. In Lanark, Paisley (still the world's largest manufacturer of cotton thread) and Falkirk these developments have left their mark in the shape of old factories and exhibitions.

In 1707 Glasgow was still only a town of some 13,000 inhabitants, but by 1830 had mushroomed to 200,000 as a result of the unplanned growth of industry and the arrival of work-hungry Irish in their thousands. Even in 1773 Edinburgh attracted five times as many nobility and gentry, while Glasgow was founded upon the skill and enterprise of her merchants and manufacturers, reflected by the Georgian elegance and Victorian self-confidence of

Above: Glasgow University, an architect's drawing.

Right: Sailing on the Clyde.

parts of the city. In 1727 Daniel Defoe could describe Glasgow as 'the cleanest, and most beautiful and best built city in Britain, London excepted', but it was not long before the Georgian streets to the south of the Clyde were engulfed by the sprawling slums of the Gorbals — a bitter legacy from the industrial past with which the city is still grappling.

Glasgow is not the most obviously attractive of cities for the visitor, but there are interesting things to see, notably the smoke-blackened, but beautiful Gothic cathedral; its oldest house, Provand's Lordship (1471), nearby, containing a fine collection of pictures, tapestry and furniture; the university and world-famous Art Gallery and Museum in Kelvingrove Park; the Hunterian, Transport and Old Glasgow museums; and Pollok House, with its remarkable Spanish paintings, soon to house the splendid Burrell Collection.

There are certain dishes which are so universally popular that they cannot properly be said to belong to one region rather than another.

Fair fa' your honest, sonsie face
Great chieftain o' the puddin race!

wrote Burns of haggis, while the other great national dish he described as 'The halesome parritch, chief o' Scotia's food'.

Porridge is one of a number of ways of serving the oatmeal — others are Aigar Brose and Gruel — which Marian McNeill once called the 'backbone of many a sturdy Scotsman'. No self-respecting Scot would make it with 'porridge oats', but would preferably use Midlothian oats, fresh spring water and a special pan reserved for cooking it. It was traditionally spoken of in the plural, and the custom was to stand whilst supping 'them'.

To those who regard haggis as a music hall joke or 'look down wi' sneerin', scornfu' view on sic a denner', we would point out that it has a taste much resembling the delicate French *boudin blanc*; at one time, in fact, it was thought that it originated in France, but this is almost certainly untrue, since in the days of the Auld Alliance *'le pain bénit d'Ecosse'* was regularly sent to exiles abroad. It is traditionally eaten at Burns Suppers, St. Andrew's Night dinners and at Hogmanay (the New Year), when it is sometimes ceremoniously piped around the table and copiously accompanied by whisky. Porridge, on the other hand, was formerly eaten with small ale.

Cock-a-leekie soup.

PORRIDGE

A recipe which that doyen of Scots cooks, Marian McNeill, describes as 'the one and only method'.

Per person:

1¼ oz (35 g) oatmeal   1 salt-spoon salt
1 breakfast cup (3 dl) water

Bring the water to the boil in a saucepan, then add the oatmeal with the left hand, letting it drop like a steady rain, meanwhile stirring briskly with the right hand, sunwise — for luck. Once the porridge is boiling steadily, draw it to the side of the stove and put on the lid. Let it cook there for 20 to 30 minutes, and do not add the salt for at least 10 minutes, since it has a tendency to harden the meal and prevent its swelling. Ladle straight into soup plates and serve with small individual bowls of cream, milk or buttermilk. Each spoonful of porridge, which should be very hot, is dipped in the cream or milk, which should be quite cold, before it is conveyed to the mouth.

The purist Miss McNeill adds: 'Children often like a layer of sugar, honey, syrup, or treacle, or of raw oatmeal on top. A morsel of butter in the centre of the plate agrees with some digestions better than milk.'

42

COCK-A-LEEKIE

One of the best known and most nourishing of Scots soups. The prunes are sometimes added to give a little sweetness.

To serve 6 :

1 boiling fowl, trussed	Bouquet garni
1 lb (½ kg) leeks, split lengthwise	Salt and pepper
1 lb (½ kg) onions, finely chopped	¼ lb (110 g) soaked prunes (optional)
	2 oz (60 g) rice (optional)

Put the bird into a large saucepan, cover it with water, bring to the boil and skim. Split the leeks into four lengths, then wash and cut them into small pieces, reserving the greenest parts. Add to the saucepan, together with the onions, bouquet garni, and salt and pepper to taste. Simmer for 2 to 3 hours, depending on the weight of the fowl, and adding a little more water if necessary. Now remove the bird, cut the meat into dice and return it to the pan with the green of the leeks and the prunes and rice, if used. Simmer for a further 15 minutes before serving.

HAGGIS AND NEEPS

Most people buy haggis ready made without enquiring too carefully how it is made. It comes in a variety of sizes, best bought from a local butcher, and should be covered with water and simmered gently for about an hour before serving. Since it tends to be a little dry, it is usually accompanied by mashed neeps (turnips) and creamed potato. It is not worth making a small haggis yourself; for those who wish to make a large one the hard way, the following recipe is reliable.

Serves 10 :

Sheep's stomach bag, scraped and steeped overnight	1 lb (½ kg) pinhead oatmeal, toasted (see page 122)
Sheep's pluck (lights or lungs, heart and liver)	1–2 oz (25–50 g) salt
¼ lb (110 g) shredded suet	1 teaspoon black pepper
1 lb (½ kg) chopped onions	1 teaspoon mixed herbs

Haggis, the traditional dish of Scotland.

Wash the pluck and boil in a large saucepan for about 2 hours. Leave to cool in the water overnight, then remove. Chop the heart, lights and liver (the very best haggis is made with deer's liver) and mix with the other ingredients, together with 1 pint (6 dl) of the cooking liquid. Fill the bag rather more than half full or make smaller ones. Press out the air, sew up and prick well – or, in the words of the poet, 'bounce, goes the bag, and covers me all over'. Simmer for about 3 hours before serving.

As an alternative to the mashed neeps and potatoes, haggis is served with Clapshot (see page 141) – and, of course, with a glass of whisky.

THE EAST

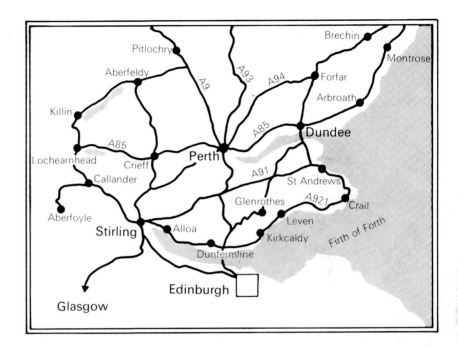

The Lowlands of the east and centre are in many ways the cradle of Scotland as it exists today. After Kenneth MacAlpin had united his western kingdom of Dalriada with Pictland to the east in A.D. 843, he made Perth the capital, and so it continued until the middle of the fifteenth century. Scotland's kings were crowned at Scone nearby, while St. Andrews remained the country's premier diocese until the Reformation.

There is no obvious route around the region as a whole, and for many visitors it is an area to be crossed *en route* for the Highlands, to which one of the most direct approaches is by Edinburgh, the Forth Bridge, the M90 motorway, and thence by Perth and the A9 to Inverness. The best point of departure for its mountainous fringes to the north and west, bordering the Trossachs and embracing the beautiful Loch Earn and Loch Tay, is Stirling. The Kingdom of Fife, cut off both to the south and the north until the construction of the Forth and Tay bridges, lies on no through route – but St. Andrews is a must, both for golfers and those interested in Scottish history. From there (or from Perth) it is a short drive to Dundee and the glens and woods beyond.

Stirling is dominated by its castle, poised on a precipitous rock above the town and still used as a regimental headquarters. A

Stirling Castle, near which Wallace and Bruce won victories over the English.

45

favourite royal residence from the time of Alexander I in the early thirteenth century to that of Mary Queen of Scots, the castle was one of the main bones of contention with the English during the Wars of Independence; and it was hard by Stirling that Wallace and Bruce won two famous victories, the Battle of Stirling Bridge in 1297 and the Battle of Bannockburn in 1314.

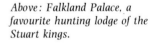

Above: Falkland Palace, a favourite hunting lodge of the Stuart kings.

Left above: Earls Hall near Leuchars, set in beautiful gardens.

Left: Glen Clova in Angus, on the fringe of the Grampians.

From Stirling the road for the Trossachs lies through Dunblane, with the ruins of its fine thirteenth-century cathedral, and the little town of Callendar, the 'Tannochbrae' of those stalwarts of television, Drs. Finlay and Cameron. Further to the east, the A822 goes by Crieff, an elegant resort on the fringe of the Highlands proper, and then by the Sma' Glen, a compendium of Highland scenery in miniature, and across the moors to the old cathedral town of Dunkeld, still well wooded as when the removal of Birnam Wood to Dunsinane spelt the fate of Shakespeare's Macbeth. Short of Dunkeld and a mile or two past Amulree, a diversion to Aberfeldy by the A826 and thence by the B864 will take you through splendid upland scenery, close to the 3546-foot Schiehallion, surely the most graceful of Scottish mountains, and along the shore of Loch Tummel — the 'Queen's View' at its eastern end and the nearby Pass of

Killiecrankie are celebrated viewpoints — before joining the A9 rather north of Pitlochry. With its many comfortable hotels, this is an excellent base for excursions; it is also the home of the well-known summer Festival Theatre.

The main A9 from Stirling to Perth passes close to Gleneagles, famous for its championship golf courses and hotel, a byword for luxury, sophisticated food and fine wines. Perth, although few relics remain of its historic past, is a gracious town with a fine esplanade flanking the River Tay and two wide parks, the North and South Inch, within its boundaries. It was on the 100-acre North Inch that an extraordinary ritual combat took place in 1396 to settle a quarrel between the Clan Chattan and the Clan Kay; the Clan Chattan being one man short of their thirty champions, the issue was effectively settled in their favour when they were joined by the redoubtable Hal o' the Wynd, a bandy-legged Perth blacksmith. The many antique shops and bookshops of present-day Perth are a happy hunting ground for visitors.

The Pass of Killiekrankie in Perthshire, where 'Bonnie Dundee' was killed while fighting the Covenanters.

A street in Culross, a well-preserved example of a sixteenth-century Scottish town.

Scone Palace, three miles to the north, was largely destroyed by a mob from Perth gripped with religious fervour after John Knox's inflammatory sermon in 1559. The existing castellated palace dates from 1803 and contains collections of furniture and *objets d'art* – the famous coronation Stone of Scone was seized and removed to Westminster Abbey by Edward I in 1296.

Fife falls into two distinct areas: the industrial south west with its coal mines and textile manufactories, extending from Kincardine on the River Forth to Leven along the coast to the east; and the north east, with its low hills, belts of woodland and prosperous farms.

Within the industrial belt are two places of particular historical interest: Culross and Dunfermline. Culross, incongruously sited across the Firth of Forth from the flaring stacks of the great petroleum refinery at Grangemouth, is perhaps the most perfect example of a small Scottish town of the sixteenth and seventeenth centuries. Its preservation was one of the first projects of the National Trust for Scotland: since 1931 the Palace, with its crow-stepped gables, pantiled roofs and painted ceilings, has been restored; causeways have been relaid with cobbles; and some seventeen houses carefully renovated.

Falkland Palace, from Scotland Illustrated, *1853.*

At Dunfermline, six miles to the east, is the splendid Benedictine abbey founded by Queen Margaret, wife of Malcolm Canmore; the nave is a particularly fine example of Norman work. During building works in 1818 Robert the Bruce's coffin was discovered here; his body was reinterred in the choir, and the grave is marked by a modern brass plate. Dunfermline was the birthplace of Andrew Carnegie, perhaps the best known of all Scots emigrants, who founded a vast steel business in Pittsburgh and later established the Trusts, still administered from Dunfermline, which have done so much for both his native town and education in Scotland.

To the north of Dunfermline, beyond the industrialized area and below the long profile of the Lomond Hills, lies Loch Leven, known by fishermen for its pink trout and more generally because it was in the castle on an islet in the loch that Mary Queen of Scots was imprisoned in 1567 after her defeat at Carberry Hill. It was here that she signed a deed of abdication in favour of her son, James VI, later escaping with the help of the eighteen-year-old William Douglas, the son of her jailer — only to suffer final defeat at Langside thirteen days later.

Falkland Palace on the eastern side of the Lomonds, off the A91 from Kinross to St. Andrews, has happier asssociations with Queen Mary and was a favourite seat of the Scottish court from the early sixteenth century onwards because of the good hunting in the forests which then surrounded it. Severely damaged by Cromwell's troops in 1645, the southern wing was restored by the Marquess of Bute, hereditary keeper, in 1887 and is still used by the family. One of the most attractive of Scotland's smaller palaces, it contains some fine Flemish tapestries, and the royal apartments in the damaged east wing have been restored by the National Trust for Scotland and furnished in period. The beautiful walled flower garden contains a royal tennis court, the oldest in Scotland (1539) and still in use.

Right: The Royal Tennis Court at Falkland Palace, the oldest in Scotland and still in use.

Below: Falkland Palace and its garden.

St. Andrews, 'a little city, worn and grey', is famous beyond its size, since it is at once the Canterbury and the Oxford of Scotland and hallowed by golfers for its Old Course (one of four) and as the seat of the Royal and Ancient Golf Club. 'With myself,' wrote Andrew Lang, 'it was a case of love at first sight, as soon as I found myself under the grey sky and beheld the white flame of the breakers charging over the brown wet barrier of the pier.' It is, in fact, a place miraculously unspoilt and one of the richest in Scotland in historic buildings.

Of these, the most impressive is the great roofless cathedral overlooking the sea, founded in 1160 and consecrated in the presence of Robert the Bruce in 1318. No fewer than thirty-six bishops and eight archbishops, one of them a cardinal, ruled over it before the Reformation. Further along the shore, the castle served as episcopal palace, fortress and state prison. Following the murder

Above: A nineteenth-century aquatint of St. Andrews, showing the pier and ruins of the cathedral and castle in the background.

Right: The lantern tower of the ruined St. Andrews Cathedral.

of Protestant martyrs, it was here that Cardinal David Beaton was himself murdered in 1547 and that John Knox took refuge and surrendered to the French fleet.

During the Wars of Independence Scots were effectively debarred from studying in England and many went abroad, especially to Paris. To remedy this, Henry Wardlaw, Bishop of St. Andrews, founded a university in 1412, the first in Scotland — it was followed by those at Glasgow (1450), Aberdeen (1495) and Edinburgh (1582). Thereafter, many famous Scots studied in St. Andrews, including the Admirable Crichton, George Buchanan, Andrew Melville, Napier of Merchiston, the Marquess of Montrose and probably John Knox. Among the historic University buildings which survive are St. Salvator's Chapel, and parts of the colleges of St. Leonard's and St. Mary's and of the Old Library.

Below: The Old Library, St. Andrews University.

Below right: Students in their gowns on the pier at St. Andrews after Sunday service.

Other buildings of historic interest are the West Port, one of the few remaining Scots city gates, Queen Mary's House and the House of the Knights Templars. The traditional Lammas Market, held in the streets during August, and the Byre Theatre, where a professional company presents plays, many of local interest, are both popular with visitors.

Along the coast to the south of St. Andrews in the unspoilt East Neuk ('nook') are the charming fishing villages of Crail, Anstruther, Pittenweem and St. Monans, with narrow streets descending precipitously to small harbours ringed by crow-stepped houses of the seventeenth and eighteenth centuries – almost Mediterranean-like when seen on a sunny day. Anstruther was an important herring port until the shoals swam further afield, and is now appropriately the home of the well-arranged Scottish Fisheries Museum and the North Carr Lightship. Further down the Firth of Forth, Elie and Lower Largo are pleasant seaside resorts; Methil, Kirkaldy (the birthplace of Adam Smith and centre of the linoleum industry) and Burntisland once thrived on the shipment of coal from the Fife mines and have seen something of a revival as bases for the North Sea oil industry and the construction of drilling platforms.

*Above: The harbour at
St. Monans.*

*Right: The harbour and Customs
House at Crail on the Fife coast.*

St. Andrews, former ecclesiastical capital of Scotland, from Scotland Illustrated, *1853.*

Dundee, half-an-hour's drive north of St. Andrews by the Tay Road Bridge and picturesquely situated on low hills rising from the Tay estuary, is Scotland's third city. Massively reconstructed and extended during the Victorian era, the ancient Royal Burgh has little to show of its historic past. For long known as the city of jam, jute and journalism, it is a place which has seen great economic vicissitudes – at one time, when the women went out to work in the jute mills, their stay-at-home husbands were known as 'pot-minders'. The original two-mile-long Tay railway bridge, traversed with such *éclat* by Queen Victoria's royal train in June 1878 three weeks after its opening, was later the scene of one of the worst disasters in British railway history, when it collapsed into the river during a tremendous gale in December 1879 with the loss of a passing train and all its eighty passengers.

The first Tay Railway Bridge, blown down during a storm in 1879.

Golf

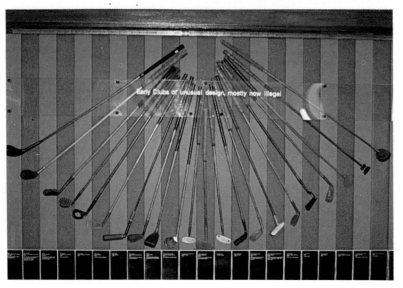

Previous page: The mountain course at Killin. Left above: Tom Morris, Keeper of the St. Andrews links. Left: Early clubs of unusual design, now mostly illegal.

The origins of golf are heatedly debated. The game took its name from the German *kolbe*, meaning 'a club'. It evolved slowly in the Low Countries and Scotland during the Middle Ages, but it was in Scotland that the game emerged in its present form.

The first written reference to golf, spelt as 'gowf' or 'goff', was in a declaration of James II of Scotland in 1457 that it be 'utterly cryit doune and nocht usit' because it led his subjects to neglect their archery practice. Later Scots

Above: The Golfers, a nineteenth-century portrait group by Charles Lees, R.S.A. Right: The 18th hole and Royal and Ancient Golf Club, St. Andrews.

kings became devotees of the game, and when James VI became James I of England he inaugurated a course on Blackheath common.

Properly constituted Golf Clubs took shape with the offer of trophies for annual competitions, the first of which was the Silver Club of 1744, presented by the Magistrates of the City of Edinburgh and to be played for by the Honourable Company of Golfers on the links of Leith. The formation of the Royal and Ancient Club in St. Andrews, now the

legislative authority for the game, followed in 1754, and the growing pre-eminence of St. Andrews eventually led to universal acceptance of the 18-hole course.

It was the seaside courses of Scotland which both gave rise to the name 'links' and in whose natural hazards the origins of bunkers are to be found.

The evolution of golf clubs, from the wooden-shafted to the present stainless steel, and of balls, from the 'featheries' and gutta-percha to the modern rubber-cored, may be studied in the private collection of the Royal and Ancient Club or in golf museums such as Camperdown House in Dundee.

Today there are over 350 courses in Scotland where visitors may play. Golf has always been devoid of snobbery in Scotland and on the many public courses, including the famous Old Course at St. Andrews, there is no formality except to pay the fee. On private courses it is sometimes helpful for the visitor to bring a letter of introduction from his local club.

Left above: The Man who Missed the Ball on the First Tee at St. Andrews, *by H. M. Bateman. Left below: The Highland course at Kingussie. Right: The Silver Club of 1744. Below: The links at St. Andrews.*

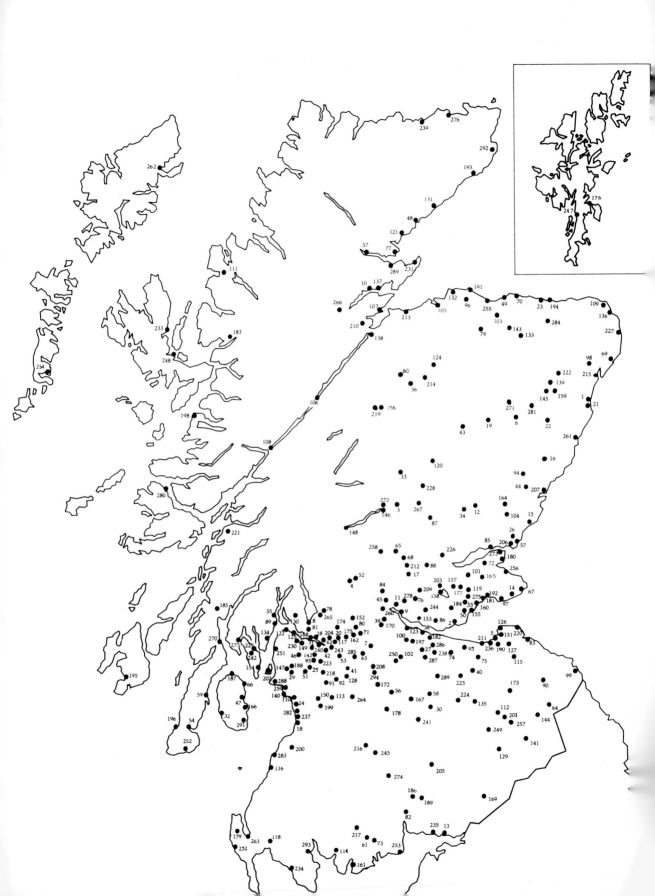

Golf Courses in Scotland

1 Aberdeen (9)
2 Aberdour
3 Aberfeldy*
4 Aberfoyle*
5 Aberlady
6 Aboyne (2)
7 Airdrie (2)
8 Alexandria
9 Alloa
10 Alness*
11 Alva*
12 Alyth
13 Annan
14 Anstruther*
15 Arbroath
16 Auchinblae
17 Auchterarder (4)
18 Ayr (3)
19 Ballater
20 Balmore
21 Balnagask
22 Banchory
23 Banff
24 Barassie
25 Barrhead
26 Barry
27 Bathgate
28 Bearsden (3)
29 Beith
30 Biggar (2)
31 Bishopton
32 Blackwaterfoot
33 Blair Atholl (2)
34 Blairgowrie
35 Blairmore
36 Boat of Garten
37 Bonar Bridge
38 Bo'ness
39 Bonnybridge*
40 Bonnyrigg
41 Bothwell
42 Braehead
43 Braemar
44 Brechin
45 Bridge of Allan
46 Bridge of Weir (2)
47 Brodick (2)
48 Brora
49 Buckie (2)
50 Burntisland
51 Caldwell
52 Callander
53 Cambuslang (2)
54 Campbeltown
55 Cardenden*
56 Carluke
57 Carnoustie (5)
58 Carnwath
59 Carradale*
60 Carrbridge
61 Castle Douglas*
62 Clydebank (2)
63 Coatbridge (2)
64 Coldstream

65 Comrie*
66 Corrie
67 Crail
68 Crieff
69 Cruden Bay
70 Cullen
71 Cumbernauld
72 Cupar*
73 Dalbeattie (2)
74 Dalmahoy
75 Dalkeith
76 Dollar
77 Dornoch
78 Drymen (2)
79 Dufftown
80 Dullatur
81 Dumbarton (2)
82 Dumfries (3)
83 Dunbar (2)
84 Dunblane
85 Dundee (3)
86 Dunferline (3)
87 Dunkeld*
88 Dunning*
89 Dunoon
90 Duns*
91 Eaglesham
92 East Kilbride (2)
93 Edinburgh (24)
94 Edzell
95 Elderslie
96 Elgin
97 Elie (2)
98 Ellon*
99 Eyemouth*
100 Falkirk (2)
101 Falkland*
102 Fauldhouse
103 Fochabers
104 Forfar
105 Forres
106 Fort Augustus*
107 Fortrose
108 Fort William
109 Fraserburgh
110 Gailes
111 Gairloch
112 Galashiels (2)
113 Galston
114 Gatehouse of Fleet*
115 Gifford*
116 Girvan
117 Glasgow (24)
118 Glenluce*
119 Glenrothes
120 Glenshee*
121 Golspie
122 Gourock
123 Grangemouth
124 Grantown-on-Spey
125 Greenock (2)
126 Gullane (5)
127 Haddington
128 Hamilton

129 Hawick (2)
130 Helensburgh
131 Helmsdale*
132 Hopeman
133 Huntly
134 Innellan*
135 Innerleithen*
136 Inverlochy
137 Invergordon*
138 Inverness (2)
139 Inverurie
140 Irvine (2)
141 Jedburgh*
142 Johnstone
143 Keith
144 Kelso*
145 Kenmay
146 Kenmore
147 Kilbirnie
148 Killin
149 Kilmacolm
150 Kilmarnock (2)
151 Kilspindie
152 Kilsyth*
153 Kincardine
154 Kingarth*
155 Kinghorn (2)
156 Kingussie
157 Kinnesswood*
158 Kinross (2)
159 Kintore*
160 Kirkcaldy (2)
161 Kirkcudbright
162 Kirkintilloch (2)
164 Kirriemuir
165 Ladybank
166 Lamlash
167 Lanark (2)
168 Langbank
169 Langholm*
170 Larbert (2)
171 Largs (2)
172 Larkhall
173 Lauder
174 Lennoxtown
175 Lenzie
176 Lerwick
177 Leslie*
178 Lesmahagow
179 Leswalt
180 Leuchars
181 Leven (4)
182 Linlithgow
183 Lochcarron
184 Lochgelly
185 Lochgilphead*
186 Lochmaben*
187 Lochranza*
188 Lochwinnoch
189 Lockerbie*
190 Longniddry
191 Lossiemouth
192 Lundin Links (3)
193 Lybster

194 Macduff
195 Machrie
196 Machrihanish
197 Maddiston
198 Mallaig
199 Mauchline
200 Maybole*
201 Melrose*
202 Millport
203 Milnathort*
204 Milngavie (5)
205 Moffat
206 Monifieth (4)
207 Montrose (5)
208 Motherwell
209 Muckhart
210 Muir of Ord
211 Musselburgh
212 Muthill*
213 Nairn (2)
214 Nethybridge*
215 Newburgh*
216 New Cumnock*
217 New Galloway*
218 Newton Mearns (2)
219 Newtonmore
220 North Berwick (3)
221 Oban
222 Old Meldrum
223 Paisley (3)
224 Peebles
225 Penicuik
226 Perth (4)
227 Peterhead
228 Pitlochry
229 Port Bannantyne
230 Port Glasgow
231 Portmahomack*
232 Portpatrick
233 Portree
234 Port William
235 Powfoot
236 Prestonpans
237 Prestwick (2)
238 Pumpherston*
239 Reay
240 Renfrew
241 Rigside*
242 Rothesay (2)
243 Rutherglen (2)

244 Saline*
245 Sanquhar*
246 Scarinish
247 Scalloway
248 Sconser
249 Selkirk*
250 Shotts
251 Skelmorlie
252 Southen
253 Southerness
254 South Uist
255 Spey Bay
256 St. Andrews (5)
257 St. Boswells*
258 St. Fillans*
259 Stevenston
260 Stirling
261 Stonehaven
262 Stornoway
263 Stranraer
264 Strathaven
265 Strathendrick
266 Strathpeffer
267 Strathtay*
269 Tain
270 Tarbert*
271 Tarland
272 Taymouth
273 Tayport
274 Thornhill*
275 Thornton
276 Thurso
277 Tighnabruaich*
278 Tillicoultry*
279 Tiree
280 Tobermory*
281 Torphins*
282 Troon (5)
283 Turnberry (4)
284 Turriff
285 Uddingston
286 Uphall
287 West Calder
288 West Kilbride
289 West Linton
291 Whiting Bay
292 Wick
293 Wigtown
294 Wishaw

There are also 18-hole courses at Kirkwall and Stromness in Orkney.

Places with more than one course have the number of courses in brackets. An asterisk (*) denotes a 9-hole course. For full details see the Scottish Tourist Board's *Scotland Home of Golf*.

63

Some dozen miles north of Dundee lies the great turreted castle of Glamis, dating from the seventeenth century, but begun much earlier. With its celebrated ghost and sealed room, open only to the firstborn of the family, it is one of the most romantic of great baronial houses and contains extensive collections of armour, furniture and tapestries. Glamis was the childhood home of Queen Elizabeth the Queen Mother, and Princess Margaret was born there in 1930.

The small town of Kirriemuir to the north was the 'Thrums' of Sir James Barrie's early books; and the little stone house in which this most whimsical of writers was born — he was, of course, the author of *Peter Pan* — is now maintained as a museum by the National Trust for Scotland. Glen Clova, beyond Kirriemuir on the edge of the Grampians, with its swift-flowing burn and sheets of yellow broom in early summer, is one of the most delightful in this foothill country.

Whitefish is caught off the east coast in great variety; and you will find trays of filleted plaice, lemon sole, dab, herring and haddock in any fishmonger. The small fillets of fresh haddock are especially delicious; and Arbroath, to the north of Dundee, makes a speciality of smoking haddock, either on the bone as Finnan haddock, as golden fillets or as that most delicate of smoked fish, Arbroath Smokies. These are lightly cured in a small brick kiln (and should, if possible, be eaten freshly smoked) by hanging up the whole fish in couples over smouldering hardwood chips.

The small ports along the Fife coast are mainly occupied with the inshore fishing of lobsters, crabs and prawns, magnificent when you can buy them – but most of the catch is frozen or sent to the salt water tanks at Eyemouth in Berwickshire prior to its export to France and Spain. The East Neuk is now making a name for itself among gastronomes. David Keith's Cellar in Anstruther was among the best restaurants in Scotland, and seafood is still well prepared at the Crusoe Hotel, Lower Largo; the Anchor Inn, Pittenweem; and the Smuggler's Inn, Anstruther.

Tay salmon is world famous, and the local trout is also excellent.

Fife and Angus are well known for their raspberry farms. Much of the fruit goes for jam making, but there are plenty of places where you may pick it yourself during the season.

The bakeries of such towns as Perth, Dundee and St. Andrews are unrivalled for their fresh crusty bread, currant loaves, morning rolls, scones, baps, shortbread and profusion of cakes and biscuits. Forfar bridies, pastry turn-overs filled with seasoned diced steak, sometimes flavoured with onions, and baked to a golden brown, are now popular throughout Scotland.

Left: Cumulus gathering over Glen Clova.

Below: Scots seafood from the West Coast.

STOVIES

An old Scots vegetable dish. Originally served alone, it goes well with cold meat.

2 lb (1 kg) potatoes	Salt and pepper
2–3 oz (60–90 g) butter	White stock
1 lb (½ kg) onions, sliced	

Peel and slice the potatoes. Melt most of the butter in a pan and add the onions, sweating them for a few minutes. Add the potatoes and season, then pour about half an inch of stock into the pan. Dot the top with a little more butter, bring to the boil and cover. Simmer very gently for about 1 hour, shaking occasionally so that the mixture does not stick to the bottom of the pan. Ten or 15 minutes before the potatoes are ready a little cooked and minced bacon, beef or chicken may be added.

ARBROATH SMOKIES

Smokies may be eaten cold. Alternatively, remove the heads and tails, place the smokies in about ½-inch of water in a large frying pan, cover and bring to the boil. Simmer for about 10 minutes until they are really hot, then remove them with a slotted spoon and put on a hot plate. Split them down the middle and take out the backbone. Season with freshly-ground pepper, dot with butter, then close the fish and serve at once, since they cool quickly.

TROUT MONTROSE

4 fresh trout, cleaned
1 oz (30 g) flour, with
   salt and pepper
Mixed butter and oil for
   frying
½ lb (225 g) shallots,
   finely chopped

½ lb (225 g) mushrooms
½ lb (225 g) tomatoes,
   peeled and chopped
1 fl oz (30 ml) whisky
1 teaspoon capers
1 teaspoon chopped dill
1 teaspoon chopped parsley

Dredge the trout in the seasoned flour. Heat the mixed butter and oil in a large frying pan and fry the fish slowly for 7 to 8 minutes on each side depending on size, turning them once only. Remove to a warm dish and keep hot. Now add the shallots, mushrooms and tomatoes to the frying pan. Fry for a few minutes and then add the whisky, capers, dill and parsley. Check the seasoning, cook a little longer until soft, then pour over the fish. Serve with a sprinkling of parsley on top.

PETTICOAT TAILS

Crisp, biscuit-like cakes, sometimes attributed to Mary Queen of Scots.

4 oz (120 g) butter
3 oz (90 g) icing sugar

6 oz (170 g) flour

Cream the butter and sugar together and knead in the flour. Roll out thinly on a floured board, then place an inverted dinner plate on top and trim off the edge with a pastry-cutter. Cut a round from the centre with a wine glass and divide the outer circle into radial strips. Prick with a fork and pinch around the edge. Bake in a very moderate oven (325°F, Mark 3) for 30 to 40 minutes. Dust with caster sugar and serve with the small round in the middle and the tails arranged around it so as to resemble an old hooped petticoat.

ARGYLL AND THE WEST

If it was in the Lowlands of the east that the pattern of Scottish history took shape in mediaeval and Reformation times, it was in Argyll ('The Coast of the Gaels') that the Scotti from Ireland founded their first capital at Dunadd, bringing with them the Stone of Destiny, and here too that their missionaries began their evangelizing work in the sixth century. It was probably from the later Dalriadic capital of Dunstaffnage near present-day Oban that Kenneth MacAlpin mounted his campaign against the Picts before transferring his court and the Stone of Destiny to Scone.

Argyll, now absorbed into the modern region of Strathclyde, used to embrace the mainland from Loch Shiel and Fort William in the north to the Clyde in the south and included the Inner Hebrides, described in Chapter 7. Beyond its eastern boundary lie Loch Lomond and the Trossachs. It is a region of mountains deeply penetrated by great sea lochs, and to see all of it involves long detours and returning on one's tracks. From Glasgow, the most scenic approach is by the A82 along the western shore of Loch Lomond or by car ferry from Gourock to Dunoon in the beautiful Cowal Peninsula.

Oban and its bay.

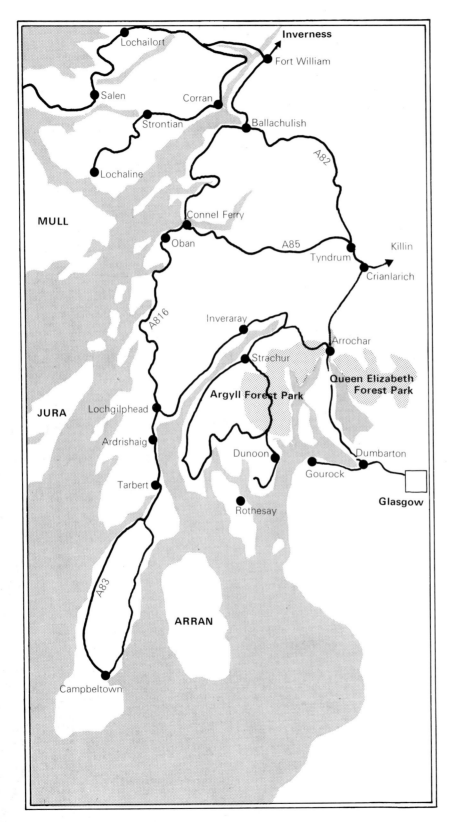

The district of the Trossachs, lying north of Aberfoyle and east of Callendar and including Lochs Ard, Chon, Venacher, Achray, Katrine and Arklet, is among the most famous in Scotland for its scenery. Its wooded gorges, clothed with oak, birch, mountain ash, heather and foxgloves, were the lair of the early eighteenth-century freebooter, Rob Roy Macgregor, the hero of Scott's *Rob Roy*, and also supplied a romantic setting for another of his novels, *The Lady of the Lake*. The steamer which plies Loch Katrine in the summer is named the SS *Sir Walter Scott* in his honour. Further west, beyond the Queen Elizabeth Forest Park and the heights of Ben Vrackie and Ben Lomond, Loch Lomond with its wooded islands is the largest stretch of inland water in the British Isles. A favourite place for excursions from Glasgow, it too may be explored by steamer; the *Maid of the Loch* sails during May to September from Balloch at the south end to Tarbet and Inversnaid towards the north.

Loch Katrine in the Trossachs, with the pleasure steamer The Lady of the Lake *in the background.*

From Tarbet the A82 and A85 make a wide northern sweep across high moorland through Crianlarich and Dalmally to Oban on the coast. Along the route and by the shore of the lovely Loch Awe is the Cruachan hydroelectric plant, where there is a Visitor Centre and minibuses will take you through a tunnel two-thirds of a mile long to the power station itself, deep in the heart of the mountain. To see Loch Awe at its best, you must make a diversion, branching left after Dalmally for Portsonachan and following the narrow and hilly B840 through the woods on its western shore.

Oban, pleasantly situated at the foot of a horseshoe bay and dominated by the circular McCaig's Folly on the hill above, is one of the railheads of the single-track line from Glasgow and a thriving little town, full of tourists in summer. It offers the visitor a swimming pool, golf, sailing and fishing; and its busy harbour is the point of departure for ferries to Mull, Coll, Tiree, Colonsay and the Outer Hebrides.

Above: Sunset over Oban.

Right: The lonely Rannoch Moor.

Fishing

A typical sight in the lobby of Scots fishing hotels is the large brass scales, where the angler deposits his catch after a day on river or loch. Scotland affords splendid scope for the fisherman, whether he is interested in game fishing, coarse fishing or sea angling. Apart from the famous salmon and trout rivers,

Left: Fly-fishing in Loch Restil. Above: Fishermen by Loch Maree.

such as the Tweed, Tay and Spey where the cost of a beat may run to hundreds of pounds a week, there are literally thousands of rivers, streams and lochs where freshwater fishing may be enjoyed for a very modest charge. The best times to fish are often in the spring, early summer and autumn, when the hotels have more room and offer special off-season prices.

The intending visitor should obtain a copy of the Scottish

Tourist Board's *Angler's Guide to Scottish Waters*, which, apart from its very comprehensive list of fishing waters, supplies a great deal of practical information about local regulations, dates of close seasons, angling societies and the most suitable tackle, both for freshwater fishing and sea angling.

It is important to know that there is no public right of fishing in fresh water. A permit must be obtained locally from the landowner on

Opposite page: On the River Tay, one of the great salmon rivers. Left: The last of a day by the sea-shore. Below: Giant skate caught in Little Loch Broom.

whose property the water lies; in many cases the hotels can offer fishing facilities.

There is a close season for fishing salmon and sea trout. This varies according to the districts, but in general rod fishing is not allowed between 1 November and mid-February, nor may these fish be caught during the twenty-four hours of Sunday. They may not be taken in fresh water except by net and coble or single rod and line, and in the north and west of Scotland salmon angling is generally limited to fly-fishing.

Since trout are more abundant the regulations are not so strict, but there is a statutory close season between 7 October and 4 March, and although Sunday fishing is allowed, it is discouraged in some districts. Rainbow trout are not native to Scotland and, like coarse fish, they may be taken at any time of year — with the proprietor's permission.

Although Scotland is best known for its game fishing, there is good sport to be had (especially in the

Left: Setting a lobster pot off Pladda in the Hebrides. Below: Sea angling in the Clyde.

lesser-known rivers, lochs, canals and reservoirs of the south) in fishing for bream, carp, eel, roach, perch, powan and pike. If you catch a fish of exceptional size, the Scottish Record Coarse Fish Committee, 63 Lauderdale Gardens, Glasgow G12 9QU, would be interested to hear. The present record for a pike is 31 lb 7 oz.

There are no restrictions on fishing for white fish in the sea – though fish of less than certain sizes must be returned – and no permit is required. Sea angling has become increasingly popular, and tackle and boats are available at many centres along the coast. Details of festivals and competitions may be obtained from the Scottish Federation of Sea Anglers, 8 Frederick Street, Edinburgh EH2 2HB. The Federation maintains a list of record catches, headed at the

*Above: The fishing quarter in St.
Andrews, calotype c. 1845 by
D. O. Hill and Robert Adamson.
Right: A Newhaven fishwife, calotype
by D. O. Hill and Robert Adamson
c. 1845.*

moment by a skate of 226 lb 8 oz
and a halibut of 212 lb 4 oz. These
big fish come mainly from the
waters around Shetland and Orkney,
but there are tope and sharks in
Luce Bay to the south of Galloway,
and haddock and cod of exceptional
size have been caught in the Firth
of Clyde. Anyone who is a member
of the Scottish Federation of Sea
Anglers and who, with rod and
line, catches a fish of any species of
100 lb or over is eligible for
membership of the Scottish 'Ton Up'
Club.

As regards tackle for sea angling,
large centre-pin reels and stiff solid
rods of glass or cane have largely
been abandoned in Scotland in
favour of free-running multiplying
reels and flexible hollow glass-fibre
rods. Gone too are the short stiff

rods formerly used as boat tackle, and a light, supple rod about 7 feet long is now preferred. When fishing for shark, tope, skate, halibut or big conger, a length of wire is employed to attach the hook to the trace and to act as a biting piece. In fishing from a small boat, the usual strict safety precautions must be observed.

Below: Buoys in a fishing boat at Ullapool.

The A828 from the Falls of Lora to the north, so called because of the tidal rapids at the mouth of Loch Etive, is one of the main routes to Ballachulish, Fort William and the Northern Highlands. Skirting Loch Creran, it passes through country which is Argyll at its most typical — mountainous, yet often soft, green and luxuriant, with secret woods and banks of rhododendrons, and always water: water running, falling from the hillsides, or in the level sheets of its lochs.

Glencoe, Buachaille Etive Mor.

Off to the east of Ballachulish the A82 climbs through the ill-

omened Glencoe and crosses the desolate expanse of Rannoch Moor for Tyndrum and Crianlarich, whence you may either head south for Loch Lomond or east for the beautiful glen country of Perthshire.

The Massacre of Glencoe took place on 13 February 1692. The pretext for the slaughter of the Macdonalds, who inhabited the glen, was that their chief, Macdonald of Glencoe, had unduly delayed in signing an oath of allegiance to William and Mary in place of the deposed James VII; but the Earl of Stair, who engineered their destruction, dwelt on their supposed Catholicism and gave orders in the belief that he was carrying out a 'great work of charity'. In the event, 128 soldiers under Campbell of Glenlyon, who had some days beforehand been billeted on the Macdonalds and were living on friendly terms with them, suddenly turned on their hosts. Thirty-eight of the two hundred inhabitants of the glen were murdered, most of the others escaping through the mountain passes under cover of bad weather.

The site of the massacre is marked by a monument near the 1011-foot watershed at the east end of the glen, where the barren mountains crowd closely together and the road is squeezed between

Stormy evening, Loch Fyne. It is from herring fished here that some of the best Scots kippers are made.

the wild slopes and precipices of Buachaille Etive Mor and Ben a'Chrulaiste. The best view of this sombre but beautiful glen is from 'The Study' (or 'Anvil'), a terrace above the road commanding views of the great rock wall of Aonach Eagach and the 'Three Sisters' opposite. Glencoe is now one of the most popular rock-climbing and ski centres in Scotland.

Going south from Oban along the A816, a side road at Kilninver crosses Telford's picturesque single-arched bridge, sometimes, though not quite accurately, described as the only one to 'span the Atlantic', to the little island of Seil, a popular place for summer excursions. It was from the neighbouring island of Luing that the slate was quarried for re-roofing Iona Cathedral. The area between Kilmartin and Dunadd, further south along the A816, is one of the richest in Scotland in prehistoric remains, among them Stone and Bronge Age burial cairns at Dunchraigaig, Nether Largie, Ri Cruin and Kilmartin Glebe; the Baluachraig Inscribed Rocks with ritual cup and ring engravings; and a stone circle of about 2000 B.C. at Temple Wood. The once-fortified hillock of Dunadd was the ancient capital of Celtic Dalriada from about A.D. 500 to 800; and on the rock at the top, where its kings were probably invested, is the carved figure of a boar and the sign of a footprint.

From the small holiday and market town of Lochgilphead the main road continues down the eastern side of the Knapdale peninsula to Tarbert; but the more interesting and scenic route is the B8024, which crosses to the opposite shore and continues around the tip of the peninsula, passing St. Columba's Cave, associated with his arrival in Scotland and containing an altar and carved crosses. Beyond Tarbert lies the forty-mile-long Kintyre peninsula. Campbeltown, opposite the south end of Arran, is a rather prosaic little market town engaged in fishing and the distilling of whisky; but south of it there are more early Christian remains, including the ruined chapel at Keil, where St. Columba is said to have landed on his first mission. Two footprints cut into a nearby rock commemorate his decision never to return to Ireland.

One of the most beautiful parts of Argyll is the Cowal peninsula with its sea lochs, mountains and forests, clutching the island of Bute to the south like a lobster's claw. It is most easily approached by the car ferry from Gourock to Dunoon, the popular Clyde resort. From there the A815, skirting the Holy Loch with its American submarine base, soon runs into the magnificent Argyll Forest Park and along Loch Eck, overhung by great wooded mountains. The Park, the first to be created by the Forestry Commission in 1935, covers some 60,000 acres and may be explored on foot through its many forest walks. Do not miss the Younger Botanic Garden, with its fine avenue of sequoias and colourful display of rhodo-dendrons and azaleas.

Emerging from the Park, the road next skirts the impressive Loch Fyne, rounding its northern tip to reach Inveraray, most elegant of small Highland towns, with its steamer jetty, wide streets and Georgian houses, surmounted by the graceful spire of the Episcopalian Church. It is, incidentally, a town which caters for summer visitors without vulgarization, and a good place to buy a kilt or tartan dress. Inveraray Castle, in a deer park on the outskirts, is the seat of the chiefs of the Clan Campbell, Dukes of Argyll, who, because of their support of the Covenanters and their anti-Jacobite sentiments, were so hated by many other Highlanders. Begun in 1743, the castle was built with the assistance of the Adam family, and its magnificent interiors were decorated by Robert Milne during 1772–82. It was severely damaged by fire in November 1975, although many of its paintings and other treasures were saved by estate workers and the townspeople from Inveraray. Since then the castle has been extensively restored and is now open again to visitors.

From Inveraray, you may either continue to Oban via the A819 and the north shore of Loch Awe or southwards to Lochgilphead by the western shore of Loch Fyne. At Auchindrain there is an interesting folk museum, illustrating life on a West Highland farm.   *Roast pheasant.*

The French traveller, Bartolomé Faujas de Saint Fond, had some interesting comments on the elegance of the cuisine at Inveraray Castle when he was entertained there in 1784 by the Duke of Argyll: 'The entrées, the rôti, the entrements are all served with the same variety and abundance. If the poultry be not so juicy as in Paris, one eats here in compensation hazel-hens, and above all moorfowl, delicious fish, and vegetables, the quality of which maintains the reputation of the Scottish gardeners who grew them.'

He continues with an intriguing sidelight on the custom of the ladies leaving the table after dessert and during the circulation of the port:

'Wines are the great luxury of the table in England [sic], where they drink the best and dearest that grow in France and Portugal. If the lively champagne should make its diuretic influence felt, the case is foreseen, and in the pretty corners of the room the necessary convenience is to be found. This is applied to with so little ceremony, that the person who has occasion to use it, does not even interrupt his talk during the operation. I suppose this is one of the reasons why the English ladies, who are exceedingly modest and reserved, always leave the company before the toasts are begun.'

Faujas de Saint Fond's comments on the excellence of the raw materials still stand. One might add that Loch Fyne is particularly known for its kippers, made by splitting open the plump West Coast herring, salting them and hanging them up to smoke over oak chips. There is all the difference in the world between a kipper such as this and those made artificially by the incorporation of lurid orange dye.

KIPPERS

Kippers should *not*, as so many Sassenachs think, be boiled in water. To preserve the flavour, the correct method is to lay them face to face in a frying pan without fat. Cover and cook over a gentle flame for five minutes, turning the pair, while still keeping them face to face, only once. The oil which emerges when they are heated is quite sufficient to cook them.

PHEASANT LOCH EIL

2 pheasants

Salt and pepper

3 oz (90 g) butter

$\frac{1}{4}$ pint (1$\frac{1}{2}$ dl) double cream

2 teaspoons lemon juice

Truss the pheasants with the legs pressed against the breast. Season and place in a casserole with melted butter, brushing some of it over them. Cover and cook on top of the stove for about $\frac{3}{4}$ hour. Remove the lid 10 minutes before they are done, pour the cream over them and baste frequently. Add the lemon juice and correct the seasoning before serving.

VENISON ROLL

Venison can sometimes be tough, and this is an attractive way of cooking it.

½ lb (225 g) venison flank or shoulder, minced

½ lb (225 g) venison heart, minced

½ lb (225 g) venison liver, minced

2 medium onions, finely chopped

2 or 3 tomatoes, peeled and diced

½ lb (225 g) streaky bacon, finely chopped

Grated peel of 1 lemon

1 egg

1 oz (30 g) fresh bread-crumbs

Salt and pepper

Browned crumbs

Dripping

Mix together all the ingredients, except the browned crumbs and dripping, in a large bowl. Season well and shape into a roll, sprinkling it with the browned crumbs. Now place the roll in a roasting tin with a little hot dripping. Baste and cover with foil, then bake in a moderately hot oven (375°F, Mark 5) for 2 hours. Remove the foil and place in a hot serving dish. You may either make a sauce of your own choosing to accompany the roll or serve it with a salad on the side.

ATHOLE BROSE

This potent Highland libation is credited to the Duke of Atholl, who, to capture the Earl of Ross in 1475, is said to have filled a well with whisky, honey and oatmeal, and waited until his rival was overcome. It nevertheless seems sufficient justification for including it at this point that the Brose was traditionally piped into the sergeants' mess of the Argyll and Sutherland Highlanders on Hogmanay, where a quaich was filled for each officer and sergeant.

3 oz (90 g) oatmeal

1 pint boiling water

2 tablespoons liquid heather honey

Whisky to make 1 quart

1 egg, well beaten

Pour the boiling water over the oatmeal, stir well and allow to cool. Strain off the oatmeal and dissolve the honey in the liquid, using a *silver* spoon. Add the whisky and stir in the beaten egg. Keep in a well-corked bottle and shake before using.

This is a sovereign cure for a cold and also makes an attractive sweet if a little is poured into tall glasses, topped with whipped cream, sprinkled with toasted oatmeal and served chilled.

THE NORTH EAST

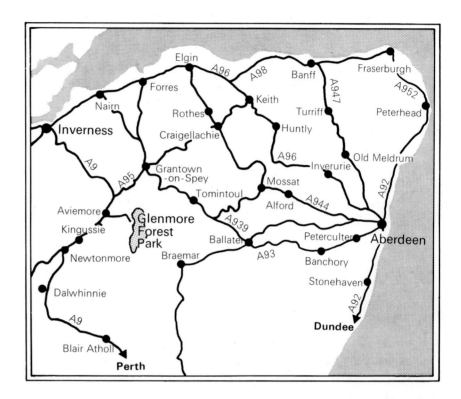

The North East is a region of contrasts. Along a fertile, low-lying coastal belt in the east are the largest fishing ports in Scotland, Stonehaven, Peterhead and Fraserburgh, with Aberdeen roughly at their centre, and a series of flourishing towns – Banff, Fochabers, Elgin, Forres and Nairn – spaced out on, or somewhat behind, the line of the Moray Firth towards Inverness. For some two hundred and fifty years, until their defeat at Aberdeen in 1562, the 'Gay Gordons' (later Marquesses of Huntly) were unchallenged masters of this part of the country; and the ruins of their great castle may be seen from the A96 between Inverness and Aberdeen at Huntly.

Inland from Deeside lies a barren expanse of moorland and mountains. The Cairngorms, with eight peaks over 4000 feet, is the highest mountain range in Britain; to the west the Monadhliath Mountains stretch to Loch Ness, while southwards the Grampians extend into Perthshire. This is the Scotland of the fishermen, climbers, skiers and nature lovers.

Northwards from Perth there are two main routes through the heart of the Highland area (and virtually no secondary roads

Above: Loch Lee, at the head of Glenesk in Angus.

Left: The ruins of Elgin Cathedral, 'The Lantern of the North'.

through much of it): the A9 to Inverness via Pitlochry (see page 45) and the A93, crossing the 2199-foot Cairnwell Pass on its way to Braemar and Aberdeen. Both roads have been much improved for the motorist. The zigzags of the Devil's Elbow on the approach to Cairnwell – where passengers once got out and helped to push the buses uphill – have been ironed out and easily graded. Steady progress is being made in converting the A9 into a double-track motorway. The leafy but dangerous bends north of Perth and Pitlochry have disappeared, and long graded sections have opened up new views. If, as with motorways in general, cuttings and embankments lack the character of the old winding road and there is an ever-increasing build up of fast-moving traffic, the A9 is an indispensable route for making distance. For visitors who wish to enjoy the scenery in more leisurely fashion, the Scottish Tourist Board publishes routes for motorists with recommended diversions.

Beyond Pitlochry, Blair Atholl is a well-kept village with the large white Scottish Baronial castle of the Dukes of Atholl on its outskirts. It contains exhibitions of weapons, family portraits and furniture; the Duke is the only British subject allowed to maintain a private army, the Atholl Highlanders, whose bagpipers are a popular attraction at the gathering held during the summer.

After crossing the 1482-foot Pass of Drumochter the A9 reaches the bleak little village of Dalwhinnie, where a fork to the left, skirting the long length of Loch Laggan, is the main access route from

A ruined window at Elgin Cathedral.

Right above: A stormy scene in the Grampians.

Right below: Pony-trekking in the Spey Valley.

the east to Fort William and the Western Highlands.

Further north along the A9 is a string of popular summer resorts and winter sports centres. At Kingussie the Highland Folk Museum ('Am Fasgadh') embraces collections of tartans, Highland dress, household utensils, farm implements, together with reconstructed cottages and mills from different parts of the Highlands. In the Highland Wildlife Park at Kincraig, a few miles further on, you can

see red deer, bison, Highland cattle and other animals in their natural surroundings. Aviemore, with its wide choice of accommodation and its Holiday Centre, offers a wide range of activities, both in summer and winter, including fishing, swimming, boating, climbing and walks in the Cairngorms, ski-ing, skating and curling. The Ski-road from Aviemore continues into the Glen More Forest Park, 12,000 acres of pine and spruce woods and mountainside with Loch Morlich at its centre, to the chairlifts and ski-tows. With its caravan sites and hostels, open all year, this is perhaps the finest area in Great Britain for wildlife, containing as it does red deer, reindeer, wildcat, golden eagle, ptarmigan and capercailzie.

Boat of Garten, six miles north of Aviemore, is of interest for the Loch Garten Nature Reserve nearby, a breeding ground for some of Scotland's rare ospreys, and as the headquarters of the Strathspey Railway Company, which is reopening part of the old Highland Railway from Aviemore to Forres, closed in 1965. When the track and stations have been restored, volunteers will once again operate steam trains over the section from Aviemore to Boat of Garten.

North of Carrbridge, the last of these Speyside resorts, the A9 crosses some twenty-five miles of open moorland to Inverness, passing the Tomatin distillery, the largest in Scotland making malt whisky. A few miles to the east of the road on the approaches to Inverness, lies Culloden Moor, much as it was when the Duke of Cumberland finally defeated Prince Charles Edward on 16 April 1746. A great memorial cairn was erected in 1881, and simple headstones along the road record the communal burial places of the different clans. A museum and Visitor Centre, featuring an audiovisual display, provide interesting background to this emotion-fraught battle, the last to be fought on British soil.

Culloden did more than crush the Jacobites; it effectively marked the end of the old patriarchal clan systen. A Disarming Act passed in 1747, besides prohibiting the carrying of arms, forbade all males, except soldiers belonging to the armed forces of the Crown, to 'wear or put on cloathes commonly called Highland Clothes this to say the Plaid, Phillibeg or Little Kilt'. The wearing of tartan in any form was proscribed under severe penalty. Although the Act soon fell into disuse and was repealed in 1782, the clans were never revived in their old close-knit form — many of the chiefs were by then more interested in developing their landholdings than in keeping together their retainers. Nevertheless, the enthusiasm of Sir Walter Scott and the visit of the tartan-clad George IV to Edinburgh in 1820 led to a furore for Highland clothes in Scotland generally; and nowadays the kilt is often regarded as the national garb. Clan Societies are a more recent development and have done much to renew links between Scotland and the descendants of the emigrants who left their native land in their thousands from the period of the Clearances onwards. The movement reached a climax in the great International Gathering of the Clans held in Edinburgh during April/May 1977.

Apart from Speyside and the Cairngorms, the most popular touring area in the Highlands of the North East is Royal Deeside — so called because of the association of Queen Victoria with Balmoral. It may be approached by the A93, either westwards from Aberdeen or northwards from Perth and Blairgowrie. Going north from Blairgowrie, the road climbs through the picturesque broken country of Glenshee to the Cairnwell Pass, the point of departure of the Glenshee chairlift for the ski slopes of the Cairnwell Mountain, and descends through the wide and beautiful Glen Clunie, with mountains looming high on either side, to Braemar.

A popular summer resort and a ski centre in winter, Braemar lies picturesquely at the junction of the Clunie and the Dee. It was here that the first Jacobite rising broke out under the Earl of Mar in 1715; the turreted seventeenth-century castle, garrisoned by English troops during the rising, was rebuilt about 1748 and is in good repair. Braemar is, however, best known for its Royal Highland Gathering, held on the first Saturday in September. The first games in Braemar were organized as a trial of strength by Malcolm Canmore in the eleventh century. The athletic events were revived in 1832 and attracted countrywide interest when in 1848 Queen Victoria and Prince Albert travelled to Aberdeen in the Royal Yacht and thence in royal procession to attend them. The following year

Left: A break in the heather for ponies and riders.

Below: Thomas Telford's bridge over the Spey at Craigellachie.

they were held at Balmoral and have enjoyed royal patronage ever since. Over the years the programme has been extended to include Highland dancing and track events as well as the traditional wrestling, putting the shot, throwing the hammer and tossing the caber, all of course accompanied by the skirl of pipes from massed bands. The Braemar Gathering is not the only one to be held in the North East; Games take place at Ballater and Aboyne, and in many other places throughout Scotland.

Balmoral, Queen Victoria's 'dear Paradise', is a massive granite building in Scots Baronial style with Germanic overtones, lying some eight miles east of Braemar along a particularly attractive stretch of the A93 threading between wooded hills and hugging the River Dee, smoothly black and swift-running or foaming among the rocks. Prince Albert, who always felt at home in Scotland, bought the estate in 1852 and helped to plan the castle, which can be glimpsed only fleetingly across the river through a hedge screening it from the road. Crathie Church, so regularly attended by the Royal Family, stands above the road; and at Ballater the trim little station, with its elegant wooden canopies, appears to await yet another royal arrival – but the track has been torn up and the rail-

A cast-iron plaque on the Craigellachie bridge.

A ski run in the Cairngorms.

The Spey near Craigellachie, famous for its salmon fishing.

way from Aberdeen is now disused. Ballater itself is a sober little summer resort; beyond it the hills recede, and past Aboyne the road emerges into undulating farmland, passing Crathes Castle, an outstanding example of a sixteenth-century Scottish tower house, before reaching Aberdeen.

Just to the west of Ballater the narrow and precipitous A939 crosses a splendid stretch of moorland and mountain on its way to Grantown-on-Spey to the north. Tomintoul, rather beyond the 2100-foot summit, is one of the highest villages in Scotland. From Grantown, another pleasant summer resort and a centre for winter sports, it is an easy run down Strathspey by the A95 (or the more picturesque B9102 to the north of the river) to Craigellachie, with its fine iron bridge, designed by Thomas Telford in 1812 and cast in Wales, and nearby Dufftown in the heart of the whisky country.

The distilleries, some fifty in number, which cluster around the hills and glens of Speyside make malt whisky. This is used for giving flavour and finesse to the standard blends, as well as being increasingly drunk on its own by connoisseurs as 'single malt'. There have been repeated attempts to produce malt whisky elsewhere, and nobody can fully explain why it is only in certain favoured areas of Scotland that it can be made successfully. Apart from local expertise a great deal has to do with the quality of the water and of the peat, which gives it its 'smoky' flavour. Large distilleries, such as Glenfarclas, between Grantown and Craig-ellachie on the A95, and Glenfiddich at Dufftown, welcome visitors without appointment. It is the pleasantest of occupations on a wet afternoon to take refuge in the warm womb-like interiors, with their alcoholic fumes and pervading aroma of mash tub and malt, to inspect the rows of burnished copper stills and to sample the whisky after its long maturation in oak casks.

The most interesting of the old Royal Burghs on the fringes of the coast to the north is the dignified stone-built town of Elgin, some fifteen miles along the A941 from Craigellachie. Its cathedral, known as the Lantern of the North, was one of the most beautiful in Scotland while still intact. Founded in 1224, it was burned by the 'Wolf of Badenoch' and his 'wyld wykked Helandmen' after his excommunication by the bishop in 1390. Subsequently rebuilt, it fell into decay after the Reformation, but much of the thirteenth-century work and the fine fifteenth-century chapter house remain. Elgin is on the main A96 from Inverness to Aberdeen, as are Nairn, Forres, Fochabers, Huntly and Inverurie, all of them places with points of interest.

Deer in the Highland Wildlife Park at Kincraig.

Clans and Tartans

Above: Glencoe, scene of the Massacre in 1692. Right: 'Bonnie Prince Charlie', the Young Pretender, by Antonio David.

It is sometimes thought that the clans of the Scottish Highlands have existed since time immemorial and are the direct successors to the tribes which inhabited Scotland before the country was united. This is not so. Their founders emerged during the period from the twelfth to the fifteenth centuries, and they were a power in the land for some four hundred years until the collapse of the system at the time of the '45 rising (see page 91). Even as late as the sixteenth century the differences between Highland and Lowland society were, as Professor

Above: The memorial cairn to the clans at Culloden. Left: The raising of the Gordon Highlanders in 1794.

T. C. Smout has written, 'mainly ones of emphasis – Highland society was based on kinship modified by feudalism, Lowland society on feudalism tempered by kinship.'

The Gaelic word *clann* simply means 'children', and the essence of the system lay in the real or supposed blood-relationship of its members to the chief and to a heroic common ancestor, sometimes mythical – the Macgregors at different periods traced their ancestry to Cormac Mac Oirbertaigh, Kenneth Macalpin (see page 8) and Pope Gregory the Great. For practical purposes the significance of the clan lay in the imperative duty of its members to support their chief with military service and food, and of the chief to support his fellow clansmen. Any other tie, economic or otherwise, took second place to clan loyalty in times of trouble.

Some of the chiefs did not in fact possess lands of their own, and their dependants were scattered on territories occupied by other clans. As might be expected, the fierce clan loyalties often led to clashes, one of the most notorious being the massacre of the Macdonalds in Glencoe in 1692 by the henchmen of Campbell of Glenlyon (see page 80). After the rallying of the clans

Clan Donald included Macdonalds of Clanranald, Macdonells of Glengarry and of Keppoch, MacIans of Ardnamurchan and Glencoe, and Macintyres.

Clan Chattan included Mackintoshes, Farquharsons, MacThomases, Macphersons, Macgillivrays, Davidsons, Shaws, &c.

CLAN MAP OF SCOTLAND

Scale of English Miles

W. & A. K. Johnston, Limited, Edinburgh & London.

Bandsmen from the Scottish regiments: (Above, l to r) Queen's Own Highlanders, Black Watch, King's Own Scottish Borderers, Black Watch. (Left, l to r) Royal Highland Fusiliers, Gordon Highlanders, King's Own Scottish Borderers. Opposite page: Sir John Sinclair in full-dress tartan attire, by Sir Henry Raeburn.

by the Young Pretender (Bonnie Prince Charlie) in 1745 and his defeat at Culloden, the power of the chiefs was broken for good.

The wearing of coloured checks or tartans was habitual in the Highlands for centuries before the '45 rebellion, but it is a moot point as to how far clan setts (or patterns) were in use before then. In its earliest form the tartan was worn in a single piece or plaid, drawn in at the waist and thrown over the shoulders. The short kilt or *feiladh-beag* had been introduced by the early seventeenth century, but did not come into general use until the beginning of the eighteenth. For

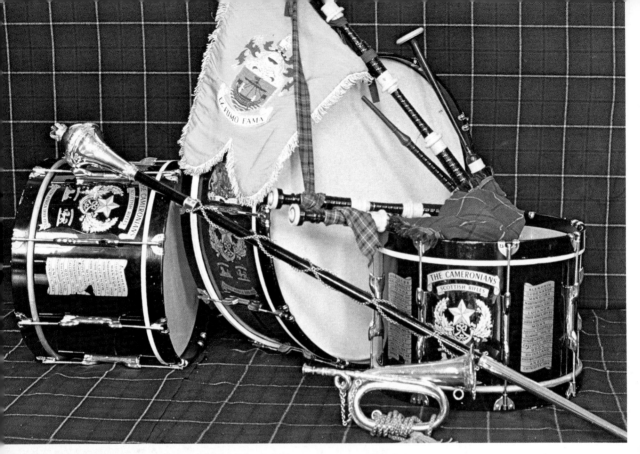

Above: Pipes and drums of the Cameronians. Left: A tartan shop in Edinburgh.

some time after the '45 the wearing of tartan was permitted only to the Highland regiments, and numerous variations of the 'Government' or Black Watch tartan were devised. The present great diversity dates from George IV's visit to Edinburgh in 1820 and his encouragement of Highland dress. By 1831 fifty-five setts were in existence, and the number has now increased to some four hundred.

It cannot seriously be claimed that all these tartans are ancient, but the revival of interest in clans and tartans and events such as the International Gathering of the Clans in 1977 have done a great deal to strengthen ties between native Scots and their kinsfolk living in North America and the Commonwealth.

The busy port of Aberdeen in the mid-1950s.

Aberdeen, the 'Granite City' and capital of the North East, is hardly the wide-open frontier town that newspaper articles on North Sea oil would suggest. There is plenty of evidence of the oil boom around the harbour and in the industrial developments on the outskirts, but the 4000 or so oil personnel have been sensibly scattered within the area; and the centre, with its wide streets flanked by great granite buildings, and the quiet university quarter of Old Aberdeen, the site of the fifteenth-century St. Machar's Cathedral and King's College (which with Marischal College forms Aberdeen University) are unspoiled. Aberdeen is also a holiday resort with wide, clean sands and a good golf course, and one of the largest fishing ports in Great Britain. The best time to visit the fish market and to see the landing and auctioning of the catch is between 7.30 and 9.30 in the morning.

Apart from its great fishing ports, the North East is the home of the famous herds of Aberdeen-Angus cattle; its farms grow a variety of fruit and vegetables; the moors and mountains provide grouse, partridge, pheasant and venison; while the Spey and the Dee are two of the most famous salmon rivers in Scotland. With all this plenty it is not surprising that the region has given birth to dozens of inventive dishes.

If you are interested in food, it is well worth stopping in Fochabers to visit Baxters of Speyside, who have built up a reputation beyond Scotland for their jams, soups and canned delicacies from the region. George Baxter, who started the business, was one of the Duke of Gordon's fifty gardeners, and the firm has rebuilt his original Victorian grocer's shop opened in 1868.

One of the pleasures of a visit to the Highlands is the opportunity to sample the malt whiskies, obtainable in such variety in almost any hotel or bar. Each has its own distinctive flavour: even Glenfiddich and Balvenie, both made by the same firm and the same methods in distilleries a stone's throw apart, are markedly different. With experience you will be able to distinguish the subtler shades of flavour between the full-flavoured Glenlivets, the smooth malts from Dufftown and nearby, and the Island malts, which are more heavily 'peated' and consequently have a more definite 'smoky' flavour. Examples of these are Laphroaig from Islay, Talisker from Skye and Highland Park from Orkney.

The ceiling of the Green Lady's Room at Crathes Castle.

Grouse shooting near Braemar.

CULLEN SKINK

A delicious fish soup from Cullen on the Moray Firth. 'Skink' is an old Scots word meaning broth.

2 lb (1 kg) Finnan haddock	2 oz (60 g) butter
1½ pint (9 dl) water	½ lb (225 g) freshly made
1 medium onion, finely	mashed potato
chopped	Salt and pepper
1½ pint (9 dl) milk	Chopped parsley for garnish

Cover the fish and onions with water in a shallow pan, bring to the boil and simmer for about 15 minutes until the fish is cooked. Take out the haddock, remove the skin and bones and return to the pan to simmer for another hour. Flake and reserve the flesh. Now strain off the fish stock from the bones and mix it with milk. Add the flaked fish, butter and mashed potatoes, stirring well until smooth in consistency. Season and serve with a sprinkling of chopped parsley, adding a little cream at the last moment if desired. One of the Finnan haddock may be replaced by an Arbroath Smokie of the same size.

HERRINGS IN OATMEAL

Herring and oatmeal were once the staple diet of the Highlanders; this combination is simple to cook and appetizing.

1 or 2 herrings per person	Salt and pepper
1 egg, beaten	Oil for frying
Finely ground oatmeal for coating	Ground parsley
	Wedges of lemon

Ask the fishmonger to clean the fish (in Scotland it is already filleted when sold). Split down the side, open out flat and remove the backbone. Dip the fillets in beaten egg, season with salt and pepper, dredge in oatmeal and leave for ½ hour so that the coating adheres firmly to the fish. Now heat a little oil in a pan and reduce the heat when it begins to smoke. Fry the fish slowly until golden-brown, remove surplus oil on kitchen paper, garnish with chopped parsley and serve very hot with wedges of lemon or with vinegar.

COLLOPS IN THE PAN

Collops, possibly a corruption of the French *escalopes*, are thin slices of beef, veal or other meat.

4 oz (120 g) finely chopped onions	2 tablespoons Madeira
2 oz (60 g) butter	2 tablespoons walnut pickle liquor
4 thin slices, each 4–6 oz (120–170 g), frying steak	3 tablespoons pickled walnuts
	Salt and pepper

Cook the onions in butter until golden brown, then add the steak and fry gently until tender. Remove the meat to a hot serving dish and meanwhile add the Madeira and walnut liquor to the pan. Stir until slightly reduced, then season the sauce and pour it over the meat. Garnish with strips of sliced pickled walnut.

MORAYSHIRE APPLES

4 cloves	2 oz (60 g) fresh beef suet
3 tablespoons (50 ml) boiling water	4 oz (120 g) soft brown sugar
3 oz (90 g) caster sugar	4 oz (120 g) medium oatmeal
1 lb (½ kg) cooking apples	2½ oz (75 g) chopped hazelnuts

Pour the water over the cloves, leave for 10 minutes to infuse, then dissolve the caster sugar, reheating if necessary. Peel, core and slice the apples and lay in an oven dish. Strain the syrup and pour it over them. Finely chop or grate the suet and mix it with half (2 oz, 60 g) of the brown sugar, the oatmeal and the hazelnuts. Spread this mixture on top of the apples and finish with a layer of the remaining brown sugar, pressing it down well. Bake in a moderately hot oven (375°F, Mark 5) for 1 hour. Serve hot with cream.

THE NORTH

The far north beyond the Great Glen, the natural divide splitting Scotland from Inverness and the Moray Firth to Fort William and Loch Linnhe, typifies Dr. Johnson's 'simplicity and wildness'. It is a region of vast and empty expanses, tumbled mountains, rolling moorland, glens, lochs and burns.

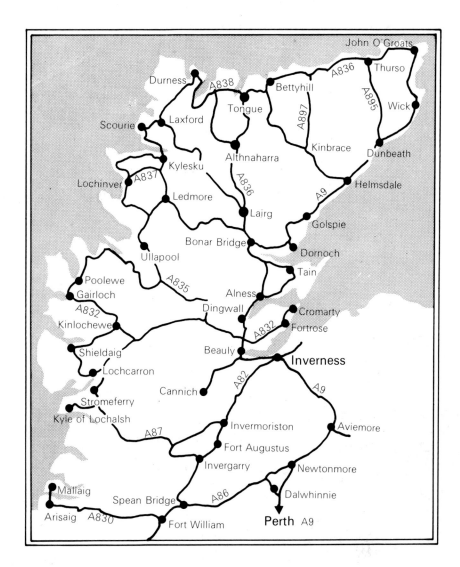

John O'Groats
Thurso
A836
A895
Wick
Durness
A838
Bettyhill
Tongue
A897
Laxford
Scourie
Kinbrace
Dunbeath
Althnaharra
Kylesku
A836
Helmsdale
Lochinver
A837
Ledmore
Lairg
A9
Bonar Bridge
Golspie
Ullapool
Dornoch
A835
Tain
Poolewe
Alness
Cromarty
Gairloch
Dingwall
Fortrose
A832
Kinlochewe
A832
Shieldaig
Beauly
Inverness
Lochcarron
Cannich
A82
Stromeferry
A9
Kyle of Lochalsh
Invermoriston
Aviemore
A87
Fort Augustus
Mallaig
Invergarry
Newtonmore
Dalwhinnie
Arisaig
A830
Spean Bridge
A86
Fort William
Perth A9

Left: A red deer stag in the Cairngorms.

Below: Glen Torridon.

There were, in fact, no roads north of Inverness or in the greater part of the west until the early nineteenth century, so that the area was completely inaccessible except to the traveller on horseback. When General Wade constructed his military roads to control the Highlanders during the Jacobite rebellions, they were all to the east of the divide. The Highland drovers who accompanied their cattle to the great trysts in Crieff and Falkirk did so on foot along the glens and over the hills; and goods were conveyed in creels on the human back, usually female, or on clumsy wooden sleds.

To remedy matters the government commissioned a report from the 'Colossus of Roads' as Southey called him, the renowned Scots engineer, Thomas Telford, as a result of which work was begun on 930 miles of roads and bridges and, in 1803, on the Caledonian Canal to link the North Sea into the Atlantic Ocean; it was completed in 1830. The sixty miles of canal link up a string of lochs, the largest being Loch Ness; but because of its twenty-nine locks — the most spectacular series of eight, known as 'Neptune's Staircase', are near the southern end — it is nowadays not much used except by pleasure craft and small cargo boats. Sailing holidays along the lochs and canal are very popular, and, who knows, you might catch a glimpse of the legendary monster.

Telford's roads, sometimes widened and straightened for motor traffic and separated by great wildernesses of mountain, moor and loch, remain the basic means of communication. A main artery is the wide A82, following the course of the Canal from Fort William to Inverness. Fort William is a lively holiday centre in summer. General Monk's fort, from which it took its name, has long since disappeared, and the town is overshadowed by the bluff bulk of Ben Nevis, the highest mountain in Great Britain and an easy climb by the main path. There are splendid views from the top, extending for some hundred miles except to the north east, where they are curtailed by the crouching mass of the Cairngorms. Westwards from Fort William the picturesque A830 passes through Glen-finnan — where the Young Pretender first raised his standard on 19 August 1745, now the venue of a Gathering and Highland Games held to commemorate the anniversary — to the fishing village of Mallaig, where it comes to a dead stop.

You may well begin a tour of the North proper by driving from Fort William along the A82 and turning left along the A87 at Invergarry along the famous Road to the Isles. Recently widened and straightened, this skirts Lochs Garry, Loyne, Cluanie and Duich, sometimes a startling blue, at others ruffled and black, or again mirror-still with an inverted image of mountain, heather and orange bracken. Pause at the head of Loch Duich to visit Eilean Donan Castle — everyone's dream of a Scots Baronial strong-hold — on a small islet, connected by a causeway with the mainland.

Its history is as romantic as its appearance, since in 1719 it was garrisoned by a Spanish expedition from Cadiz, subsequently battered into submission by an English warship. It is now the headquarters of the Clan Macrae and contains a Jacobite museum.

Some dozen miles further, Kyle of Lochalsh, the railhead of the line from Inverness and the point of departure of a car ferry for Skye, only five minutes across the water, has all the atmosphere of a frontier township. Banks, provision shops, ironmongers and drapers selling sensible clothing are crowded together by the quay, while the luxurious British Transport hotel lies poised above, as if to remind the traveller that here is a last outpost of civilization.

Previous page: Eilean Donan Castle, near Kyle of Lochalsh.

Below: Highland cattle in Glen More.

Scotch Whisky

The word 'whisky' is a corruption of the first syllable of the Gaelic *uisgebaugh*, 'water of life'. It is difficult to establish when distillation of whisky first began in Scotland, though it seems likely that the art was introduced during the Dark Ages by missionary monks from Ireland. After the passing of an excise act by the Scots Parliament in 1664, and increasingly so after the Union with England, most whisky was distilled illegally to avoid tax. The stills were thickest on the ground in Speyside, where the water and peat proved particularly suitable for making the traditional malt whisky. After the ending of illicit distilling about 1834, Speyside remained the headquarters of the industry, and in essentials its methods continue unchanged.

The barley is first malted, so converting the starch into sugar,

Right: Cutting peat. Below: A mash tun.

Above: The cooper's workshop. Left: Whisky maturing in the warehouse.

which is later fermented. This used to be done (and still is on a limited scale) in the 'pagodas' which are such a picturesque feature of the landscape. Germination is stopped by drying the grain over peat smoke, and the extent of this 'peating' is a major factor in determining the flavour of the whisky. The ground malt is extracted with pure burn water in large 'mash tuns'; the 'wort' is fermented by the addition of yeast, and is then twice distilled in copper 'pot' stills. The final step is the maturation of the young and fiery spirit for periods of years in oak casks.

As the name implies, a 'single malt' sold as such is not blended, and the characteristics of some of the different types are described on page 102. By no means all of the 130 or so different brands are available as 'single malts', and most malt whisky is in fact used for addition to 'grain' whisky to produce one of the well-known blends.

Above: Illicit still in Kintyre, Argyll.
Right: Modern 'pot' stills.

Grain whisky differs from malt in that the bulk of the starting material is not malted barley but an unmalted cereal, often maize, and distillation takes place in a large, continuously-acting Coffey or 'patent' still. The blending of malt and grain to produce a lighter spirit was pioneered by Andrew Usher in Edinburgh in about 1860. Brands such as Johnnie Walker or Grants are the end result of a complex process of blending, in which different grain whiskies and malts, in smaller amount, are mixed and matured.

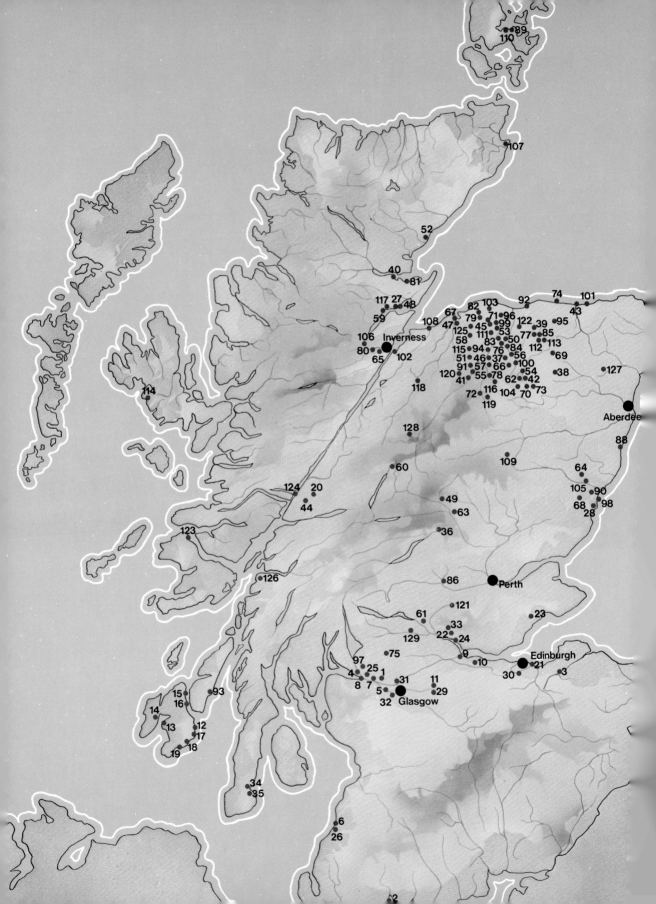

Distilleries in Scotland

Lowland malt
1 Auchentoshan
2 Bladnoch
3 Glenkinchie
4 Inverleven
5 Kinclaith
6 Ladyburn
7 Littlemill
8 Lomond
9 Rosebank
10 St Magdalene
11 Moffat

Islay malt
12 Ardbeg
13 Bowmore
14 Bruichladdich
15 Bunnahabhain
16 Caol Ila
17 Lagavulin
18 Laphroaig
19 Port Ellen

Grain
20 Ben Nevis
21 Caledonian
22 Cambus
23 Cameronbridge
24 Carsebridge
25 Dumbarton
26 Girvan
27 Invergordon
28 Lochside
29 Moffat
30 North British
31 Port Dundas
32 Strathclyde
33 North of Scotland

Campbeltown malt
34 Glen Scotia
35 Springbank

Highland malt
36 Aberfeldy
37 Aberlour-Glenlivet

38 Ardmore
39 Aultmore
40 Balblair
41 Balmenach
42 Balvenie
43 Banff
44 Ben Nevis
45 Ben Riach-Glenlivet
46 Benrinnes
47 Benromach
48 Ben Wyvis
49 Blair Athol
50 Caperdonich
51 Cardow
52 Clynelish
53 Coleburn
54 Convalmore
55 Cragganmore
56 Craigellachie
57 Dailuaine
58 Dallas Dhu
59 Dalmore
60 Dalwhinnie
61 Deanston
62 Dufftown-Glenlivet
63 Edradour
64 Fettercairn
65 Glen Albyn
66 Glenallachie
67 Glenburgie-Glenlivet
68 Glencadam
69 Glendronach
70 Glendullan
71 Glen Elgin
72 Glenfarclas-Glenlivet
73 Glenfiddich
74 Glenglassaugh
75 Glengoyne
76 Glen Grant-Glenlivet
77 Glen Keith-Glenlivet
78 Glenlivet, The
79 Glenlossie
80 Glen Mhor
81 Glenmorangie
82 Glen Moray-Glenlivet
83 Glenrothes-Glenlivet

84 Glen Spey
85 Glentauchers
86 Glenturret
87 Glenugie
88 Glenury-Royal
89 Highland Park
90 Hillside
91 Imperial
92 Inchgower
93 Isle of Jura
94 Knockando
95 Knockdhu
96 Linkwood
97 Loch Lomond
98 Lochside
99 Longmorn-Glenlivet
100 Macallan-Glenlivet
101 Macduff
102 Millburn
103 Miltonduff-Glenlivet
104 Mortlach
105 North Port
106 Ord
107 Pulteney
108 Royal Brackla
109 Royal Lochnagar
110 Scapa
111 Speyburn
112 Strathisla-Glenlivet
113 Strathmill
114 Talisker
115 Tamdhu-Glenlivet
116 Tamnavulin-Glenlivet
117 Teaninich
118 Tomatin
119 Tomintoul-Glenlivet
120 Tormore
121 Tullibardine
122 Auchroisk
123 Ledaig
124 Glenlochy
125 Mannochmore
126 Oban
127 Glen Garioch
128 Speyside
129 Glen Foyle

Above: A calm day on Loch Maree.

Left: Typical pagoda chimneys of a Scottish distillery.

Along the coast between Kyle and Ullapool to the north lies what is probably the most spectacular stretch of coastal scenery in the British Isles. The land plunges straight to the water's edge, and the sea lochs — Loch Carron, Loch Torridon, Loch Ewe, Loch Broom and the others — thrust deep between the mountains. The colours of sea and mountain change ceaselessly, season by season and hour by hour. The spring green of the mountainside gives way to the tawny purple of the heather and flaming terra cotta of the bracken in autumn, while the water, shot with peacock blues, purples and greens when the sun shines, can change within minutes to a louring black on the approach of a storm.

Following round the A890 and A832 by the shores of the dark rippling Loch Maree with its pine-clad islands, you will first come to the sandy beach and comfortable hotels of Gairloch and then to the remarkable subtropical gardens at Inverewe. Planted among pine trees on a rocky promontory, in earth carried in baskets when the garden was created in 1862, is a profusion of rhododendrons,

Himalayan lilies, giant forget-me-nots from the South Pacific and
other exotic plants. Their existence is made possible by a branch
of the Gulf Stream which washes the shore.

The A832 continues across the barren uplands of Dundonell Forest (so called, as is often the case in Scotland, from the time when it was indeed covered by the trees of the old Caledonian Forest) rimmed by the gaunt saw-teeth of An Teallach, before joining the A835 for Inverness to the south east or Ullapool, the only sizeable place along the coast to the north. A pleasant town of whitewashed houses, Ullapool was founded in 1788 by the British Fishery Society in an attempt to stem the massive emigration from Wester Ross; in summer it is now a busy holiday resort.

From Ullapool the road leads north to Ledmore, where the choice is to take the A837 through the barren Strath Oykel and thence for the east coast and Inverness, or to make for Durness via the A894 through the sombre rock-strewn wilderness of the extreme north west.

Durness is the nearest village to Cape Wrath, the most north-westerly point on the mainland, and its lighthouse, which may be visited by ferry and minibus, but not by car. Eastwards, the A838 and A836 run the whole length of the north coast to John o' Groats, first making a wide detour around the beautiful Loch Eriboll. This was one of the first areas in Scotland to be inhabited, and among other prehistoric remains there is a complete Earth-House on the west side of the loch, with a curved stair and long passage leading to a subterranean chamber. A few miles short of Bettyhill, a narrow single-track road branches south down Strath Naver, now famous for its sea-trout and salmon, but a place of grim import in the history of the Highland Clearances. It was here, in June 1814, that a factor of the Dukes of Sutherland moved in with men and dogs to evict the peasants from their crofts, setting fire to some of the houses while the families were still inside.

All over the Highlands and Islands ruined and deserted crofts stand witness to mass depopulation and the passing of a traditional way of life. Until the latter years of the eighteenth century the Highlanders had eked out a living by raising cattle, which were driven to hill pasturages during the summer months, and by growing oats and bere (an inferior form of barley) on jointly cultivated land in the straths (or valleys), carefully parcelled out into strips (or rigs), so that everyone should have a fair share of the more fertile soil. This accounts for the scattering of the crofts, which were built near the patches of land suitable for cultivation. During the eighteenth century more profitable crops were introduced in the shape of potatoes for human consumption, and turnips, as winter feed for the animals.

Another and socially disastrous innovation was large-scale sheep farming with new breeds from the Borders. The animals were voracious feeders, so that even towards the end of the sixteenth century John Knox spoke of 'the devilish custom of ejecting fifty or

Left above: Poolewe, with the dark silhouette of Inverewe Gardens among the pine trees in the background.

·Left below: Palm trees in the gardens at Inverewe.

Below: An osprey approaching its nest on Loch Garten.

117

a hundred families at a time to make way for a flock of sheep'.

The Sutherlands have perhaps borne more than their fair share of blame for the evictions. As the largest landowners in the north of Scotland, they at least made strenuous efforts to resettle the peasants in new fishing communities on the north east coast and to establish a textile industry. Emigration from the Highlands to North America, New Zealand and Australia was in the long run inevitable, because, with the recurrent failure of the potato crop by the beginning of the nineteenth century, the needs of an expanding population had by far outstripped the meagre natural resources.

Along the more easterly stretch of the A836, the road runs rather back from the sea and the scenery becomes more placid, although there are fine beaches and cliffs. The Dounreay nuclear research centre, some ten miles west of Thurso, is a strange manifestation of the twentieth century in an area so stamped by prehistory – though the stark lines of its great spherical reactor are not entirely inappropriate. An interesting exhibition is open to visitors.

The most northerly point of the mainland is not, as is often thought, John o'Groats, but Dunnet Head further to the west. Nevertheless, it is John o'Groats, with its large hotel and souvenir shops, which attracts the coaches. The views across the Pentland Firth towards Hoy, the southernmost of the Orkney Islands, to which there are day excursions by boat in summer from the little harbour, are pleasant enough; those of the Stacks, huge stone 'needles' in the sea, of nearby Duncansby Head are magnificent.

Above: Dunrobin Castle, seat of the Earls of Sutherland.

Opposite page: Rock-climbing in Inverness-shire.

Below: The atomic reactor at Dounreay.

The long road from John o'Groats towards Inverness, the A9, is completely different in character from the tortuous route along the west coast. Seldom out of sight of the sea, it is fast and easy, keeping to high ground with long views of silvery bays and jutting forelands, except for sudden and sweeping plunges into fishing villages such as Dunbeath and Helmsdale. Between the busy port of Wick, one of the railheads of the Highland line from Inverness, and Lybster, there are a number of prehistoric sites to the west of the road, among them the Grey Cairns of Camster and the Achavanish Standing Stones. Further south, Dunrobin Castle, the largest house in the North and the seat of the Earls of Sutherland, is well worth a visit. Dating from the early fifteenth century, it has been greatly extended over the years and the present building is a palace in Scots Baronial style, housing beautiful paintings, fine furniture, the antique fire-engines belonging to the estate, and relics of the Sutherland family and Queen Victoria, who stayed there.

Golspie and Brora nearby are attractive seaside resorts with good golf courses, and further south the quiet old Royal Burgh of Dornoch, with its wide square and small cathedral with some fine thirteenth-century stonework, has two excellent golf courses and miles of sands.

Beyond Dornoch the road makes a couple of wide loops inland through rich agricultural country to skirt the Dornoch and Cromarty Firths, finally running along the southern shore of the Beauly Firth to reach Inverness. The centre of rail, road and air communications for the North, Inverness is a busy, expanding and largely modern town of some 30,000 inhabitants, the capital of the Highlands.

In the past the diet of the country people in the Highlands was frugal and barely reached subsistence levels during the hard winters. The staples were gruels made from oats and barley, potatoes after their introduction from Ireland, and herring, salted in winter. This was supplemented by dairy products, but meat was not much eaten. Salmon was caught 'be or by' the proprietor's permission and was indeed so plentiful in some districts that farm servants refused to eat it more than twice a week.

The open-handed hospitality of the chiefs, both to their clansmen and visitors, was a Highland tradition. At their banquets they regularly served beef, mutton, venison, poultry and game of all kinds, washed down with ale, whisky or claret; but an English visitor, Captain E. Burt, writing of Highland cooking in 1730, described it in terms of 'inelegant and ostentatious Plenty'.

There is therefore no long tradition of fine cooking in the Highlands, and it is hardly surprising that when drawing on the game from the moors and the superb fish from the rivers, hotels should resort to methods and recipes from elsewhere. Chef Rogerson, of the Station Hotel at Inverness, has been particularly inventive in making use of local ingredients.

The making of Highland cheeses has been revived; and Mr. and Mrs. Stone welcome visitors to the creamery of their Highland Fine Cheeses at Tain on the A9, some twenty miles east of Bonar Bridge on the shores of the Dornoch Firth. Here you can see the manufacture of the traditional Highland Crowdie, a cottage cheese made without rennet by curdling the hot milk and straining off the whey. Some of these cheeses are delicately flavoured with the leaves of a wild garlic; but perhaps the most distinctive is 'Caboc', made according to a fifteenth-century family recipe from double cream with a coating of oatmeal.

Right above: The post office in the Black Isle.

Right below: An assortment of Scots cheeses from the South West, North and Orkney.

Below: The darkly rippling Loch Maree.

PARTAN BREE OR CRAB SOUP

In many parts of Scotland crabs are regarded as vermin, but this soup has for long been a favourite in Wester Ross.

1 large boiled crab
1¼ pint (6½ dl) chicken
  or veal stock
1¼ pint (6½ dl) milk
2 oz (60 g) rice

2 teaspoons anchovy essence
¼ pint (150 ml) single
  cream
Salt and pepper
Chopped parsley for garnish

Ask the fishmonger to remove the 'dead man's fingers', if you are not familiar with crabs. Remove all the meat, putting aside that from the claws.

Pour the milk and stock into a saucepan, bring to the boil, add the rice, and boil gently for 15 to 20 minutes, depending upon the type of rice, until it is tender. Now liquidize the crabmeat with the rice and broth, either in a blender or by passing it through a sieve. Return to the saucepan, add the anchovy essence, cream, the reserved meat from the claws, and salt and pepper to taste. Bring to the boil again, then remove from the fire and serve with a sprinkling of chopped parsley.

SKIRLIE

Around the Moray Firth this was traditionally served with potatoes as a nourishing and economical main dish, but it is a delicious accompaniment to roasts and hot meats of all kinds.

4 oz (120 g) suet or beef dripping
1 lb (½ kg) finely chopped onions
6 oz (170 g) medium-ground oatmeal
Salt and pepper

Melt the suet in a heavy frying pan, add the onions and fry until brown. Now add the oatmeal, cook gently for some 10 minutes more and season to taste.

Reflections in Loch Cluanie on the Road to the Isles.

ROAST GROUSE WITH WHISKY AND SKIRLIE

2 oz (60 g) salted butter
2 young grouse
8 rashers fat bacon
4 slices white bread, buttered
Skirlie (see above)
1 liqueur glass whisky

Prepare the birds by putting 1 oz (30 g) of butter inside each of them and covering the breasts with bacon rashers. Now put them on top of the slices of buttered bread in a roasting tin. Cook in a moderately hot oven (Mark 5, 375°F) for 30 to 40 minutes depending on size, and remove the bacon 10 minutes before the birds are done so as to allow the breasts to brown. Chop the bacon and stir into the Skirlie. Place the grouse on a serving dish and flame with the whisky, previously warmed, and make a gravy with the juices left in the tin. Serve on a bed of Skirlie with boiled potatoes and broccoli.

A crofter cutting peat.

CRANACHAN

Simple to make and one of the best of Scots sweets.

½ pint (3 dl) double cream
1 tablespoon caster sugar, vanilla scented
2 heaped tablespoons medium-ground oatmeal
1 tablespoon rum or brandy
¼ lb (120 g) raspberries or other berries

Beat the cream with the vanilla-scented sugar until fairly stiff. Toast the oatmeal by heating it in a heavy pan over the stove and turning with a wooden spoon until brown, then cool and mix well with the cream and rum. Put into small bowls, top with the fresh fruit and leave in the refrigerator for an hour or two, so as to chill the sweet before serving.

THE HEBRIDES

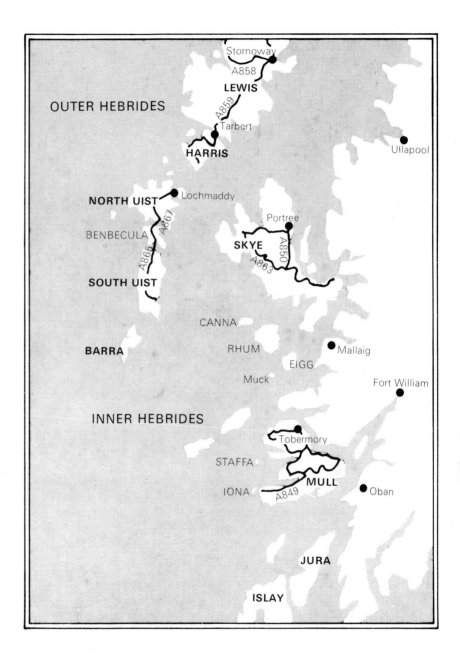

In all, the Hebrides comprise some forty to fifty islands off the west coast of Scotland, some large and inhabited and others little more than barren rocks in the Atlantic. There are two groups: the northerly chain of the Outer Hebrides, 130 miles in length from the Butt of Lewis in the north to Barra Head in the south, separated

from the mainland by some 35 miles of open sea; and the Inner Hebrides, much closer inshore, straggling south from Skye to Islay, opposite the Kintyre peninsula.

The ferry crossing of two to three hours to the Outer Hebrides seems more than a short journey to an outlying part of the British Isles. The great trailers laden with supplies and petrol, the Islanders with their suitcases and parcels, speaking English carefully as a foreign language, the bird-watchers with their windcheaters and binoculars, all suggest a voyage into the unknown. When the ferry finally manoeuvres into Lochmaddy or Tarbert, there is a brief flurry of passengers and cars, disappearing as rapidly as they came and leaving the wooden quay and huddled houses beyond to a silence broken only by the wheeling seagulls.

For many centuries the Hebrides, with Orkney and Shetland, were indeed foreign territory. The Norsemen, who arrived in their longboats in the eighth century A.D., first raided the islands and then occupied them. It was not until 1266, three years after Alexander III of Scotland had defeated King Haakon III and his fleet at Largs in Ayrshire in 1263, that the Norwegians abandoned their claim to the Hebrides. Meanwhile, in the early twelfth century, Somerled, a native chief from Morvern on the mainland had married the daughter of one of the Norse kings and gained control of many of the inner islands; and his descendant, John Macdonald of Islay (d. 1386) adopted the title of 'Lord of the Isles'. Later Lords of the Isles ruled more or less as kings in their own right until James IV annexed the Hebrides in 1489 and the title was abolished.

Left: The Cuillins, Skye, some of the most formidable mountains in Great Britain.

Below: Seals on the shore off Dunvegan.

With careful planning (because the ferries sail only on certain days of the week) it is possible to tour the Outer Hebrides by car from north to south, first crossing from Ullapool to Stornoway in Lewis and returning from Castlebay in Barra to Oban. Alternatively one may take advantage of the 'Drive Away' Car Tours organized by Caledonian MacBrayne, returning to the ship at night to sleep.

Stornoway, a lively and animated market town with a busy fishing harbour and airport, is the only sizeable place in the Outer Hebrides. Going north by the A857, the first thing that will strike you is that the island is almost completely without trees; this is true of the Outer Hebrides as a whole, the typical lanscape being windswept moorland or peat bog, interspersed with myriads of tiny lochs, dazzling blue on a sunny day. The A857 continues on to the bleak cliffs at the Butt of Lewis, but a more rewarding road is the narrow single-track A858, doubling back to Stornoway by the west coast.

Above: Evening in North Uist.

Left: Iona Cathedral, cradle of Christianity in Scotland.

Right: Handwoven Harris Tweed.

At Arnol, a few miles beyond the fork, there is a particularly interesting and well-preserved example of a Lewis 'Black House', with many of its original furnishings. The crofters built their houses of the simplest materials. A low, double dry-stone wall, filled with sand or earth, supported a wooden frame, fastened with wooden pegs or tied together with heather rope. Timber, often driftwood, was the scarcest commodity, and during the Clearances a particular grievance was that the landlords and their agents made a point of burning it. The cottages were roofed with turf sods covered with thatch, and rainwater drained away through the sand filling of the walls.

The usual plan provided for a living room, bedroom, barn and byre housed under the same roof, the cattle, which had little to eat in winter except straw, thus benefiting from the warmth. There was no chimney, and the smoke from the peat fire on a stone slab at the centre percolated slowly through the thatch, so that the cottages have been likened to 'smoking dunghills'. Furniture was of the simplest, and the box-beds were provided with a wooden top to prevent drops of water blackened with peat soot — the so-called *snighe* — from falling on the occupants. The houses were nevertheless draught-proof and cosy, the double walls, sometimes six feet thick, retaining the heat; and on her tour of the Highlands in 1803 Dorothy Wordsworth commented upon 'the beauty of the beams and rafters gleaming between the clouds of smoke. They had been crusted over and varnished by many winters till, when the firelight fell upon them, they were as glossy as black rocks on a sunny day cased in ice'.

The museum at Shawbost, a little further along the A858, created by local schoolchildren in a disused church, throws further light on Island crafts and traditional ways of life. When it was opened in 1970, the 537 villagers were operating 107 hand-looms for the manufacture of Harris tweed in their own homes, and many of the exhibits relate to spinning and weaving. This is still a flourishing cottage industry, although the yarn (from pure Scottish wool) is now spun and dyed in mills. A van distributes the bales opposite the weavers' cottages along the road, with instructions as to the type and pattern of tweed required. Knock on any door and they will be pleased to demonstrate: an expert weaver, operating his machine by treddle, can produce some eighteen yards of Harris tweed a day in the standard 29-inch width, and some will make beautiful dress and suit lengths to private order.

Another interesting exhibit at the museum is the model of the nearby Norse watermill, which has been restored and put into working order by the schoolchildren. A relic from an even earlier age is the Iron Age broch tower (see page 140), standing some 30 feet high at Dun Carloway; and set in bleak moorland to the west of the road, where it leaves the coast and heads for Stornoway, are the remarkable Standing Stones of Callanish. The huge monoliths, dating between 2000 and 1500 B.C., form a central circle with avenues extending to the four points of the compass, and are second in size and importance only to Stonehenge.

A crofter weaving tweed in Harris.

Flora Macdonald, who helped Bonnie Prince Charlie make his escape after the '45, from a painting by Allan Ramsay.

South from Stornoway, the A859 crosses into Harris (Harris and Lewis are parts of the same Long Island) and winds through the mountains and along Loch Seaforth and West Loch Tarbert to Tarbert, where a ferry runs to Lochmaddy in North Uist or to Uig in Skye. At Leverburgh in South Harris, beyond Tarbert, Lord Leverhulme unsuccessfully attempted to establish a model fishing port in 1923 after his purchase of Harris and Lewis.

North Uist and Benbecula are connected by a stone causeway; and there is a bridge from Benbecula to South Uist, so that it is possible to drive the length of the three islands from Lochmaddy to Lochoisdale in the south, where there is a ferry to Barra. Except in South Uist the land is flat and windswept, nearly half of it being covered by tiny lochs amidst the heather and peat. The bird sanctuary at Loch Druidibeg on South Uist is one of the few remaining breeding grounds of the greylag goose. South Uist is of considerable historical interest, because it was here, while on a visit to her brother, that Flora Macdonald first met the Young Pretender after his defeat at Culloden and was persuaded to take him to Skye, disguised as a servant girl.

Skye is the largest of the Hebrides apart from Lewis and Harris, and with a coast often cliff-bound and broken by sea lochs, with the bare and precipitous Cuillin Mountains and its wild and lonely moorland, it is one of the most strikingly beautiful parts of the British Isles. At Kylerhea the island so closely borders the mainland that at one time the drovers, on their way to the cattle fairs of the south, drove their animals into the water and goaded them into swimming the narrows. Today it may be reached by car ferry from Kyle of Lochalsh to Kyleakin (a five minute passage) or from Mallaig to Armadale. There is also an air service from Glasgow.

Around Armadale in the south there are luxuriant woods; and the grounds of Armadale Castle, with their rhododendrons, flowering shrubs and towering monkey-puzzle trees are subtropical in character. The castle itself, built in the early years of the nineteenth century, is under reconstruction as a centre for the Clan Macdonald. North from Armadale towards Broadford the winding one-track road soon runs into empty moorland, finally joining the wide, well-engineered A850 to Portree. At Sligachan, in a fold of the mountains at the bottom of its sea loch, the A863 forks west for Dunvegan; and the approach to Glen Brittle and the Cuillins, the barest and rockiest mountains in Britain, is by a side road doubling back to the south beyond Glen Drynoch. Often wreathed in mist and cloud, the Cuillins are for experienced climbers, and there is a hostel and climbing school in Glen Brittle.

Dunvegan Castle, north west along the A863, is Skye's most impressive building and has been the seat of the MacLeods of MacLeod — who fought so fiercely with the rival Macdonalds,

Mackinnons and others – since about 1200. Like many other castles in the west, it was originally accessible only by a portcullis giving on to the rocks and sea. If you wish to look at its interesting relics of the MacLeod family and of the Young Pretender, there is now an easier entrance by a bridge across the moat. Portree, the only place of any size on Skye, is a pleasant enough market town and tourist centre, but of no outstanding interest.

The smaller Hebridean Islands – Rhum, Eigg, Jura, Islay and the others – with their beautiful hills and coastline, their unspoilt fishing villages and unhurried pace of life, all have their charms; but it is Mull and Iona, so closely associated with St. Columba and early Christianity, that most visitors will want to visit. There are car ferries from Oban to Craignure (45 minutes) and Lochaline to Fishnish (15 minutes) and round tours by ship during the summer, which also take in Iona and sometimes skirt Staffa for a view of the extraordinary basalt columns and caves, of which the most famous is Fingal's Cave.

The coast of Mull, especially to the south and west, with its sea lochs and high cliffs, offers splendid panoramas of mountain, sky and sea; Ben More, in the south, rises to 3169 feet. The one town, Tobermory, lies on the wooded slopes of a bay which is one of the safest anchorages on the west coast and a favourite centre for yachting. It was in Tobermory Bay that the Spanish galleon *Florida* sought refuge after the defeat of the Armada in 1588. It was subsequently blown up, and frequent, but unsuccessful attempts have been made to recover its fabled treasure. In mid-July Tobermory is the venue of the Mull Highland Games, with the traditional .march led by the Chief of the Clan Maclean, and in August of the West Highland Yachting Week.

St. Columba and his followers arrived on Iona from Ireland in A.D. 563 and from there set out to convert the Picts and to spread Christianity throughout Scotland. His original monastery was destroyed by the Vikings and replaced in 1203 by a Benedictine monastery, which later served as a cathedral. The building fell into decay, and restoration was begun in the early years of the present century. Only a few minutes by ferry from the south west tip of Mull, Iona possesses other remains: the restored St. Oran's Chapel of 1080, the ruins of a thirteenth-century nunnery and the elaborately carved tenth-century St. Martin's Cross. Perhaps the last word can be left with Dr. Johnson: 'That man is little to be envied, whose patriotism would not gain force upon the plain of Marathon, or whose piety would not grow warmer among the ruins of Iona.'

Fingal's Cave, Isle of Staffa.

As in the Highlands generally, the traditional diet of the Islanders was extremely restricted (see page 120), especially in the winter when they sometimes fell back on gathering whelks and limpets from the rocks and in times of extreme scarcity on drawing the blood from their emaciated cattle. In more sophisticated form this custom – but not, of course, the drawing of blood from live animals – survives in the Black Pudding, a blood sausage obtainable all over Scotland and very similar to the Spanish *morcilla*, delicious when sliced and fried with bacon or eggs.

The people also cooked and ate the rich variety of seaweed from the coast, particularly *carrageen* (or Iceland moss), which was gathered at low tide, dried and bleached, then boiled with milk to make a sort of blancmange, flavoured with lemon or jam. Seaweed is still gathered in quantity for processing as alginate, which is used in the manufacture of ice cream.

A special mystique is attached to those typical Scots foods, porridge and bannocks (oatcakes). On Lewis and Iona porridge was thrown into the sea to ensure a good crop of seaweed. A bannock above the door prevented fairies from seizing a new-born child, while at Beltane – on the first day of May, when the cattle were driven to the upland pastures – bannocks marked with a cross on one side were rolled down the hillside. If they broke, became stuck, or finished cross upwards, it was considered an evil omen.

The whitefish industry moved to the east coast as long ago as the early nineteenth century, but excellent shellfish is caught by the boats from the numerous and picturesque little ports in the west.

Very characterful and full-flavoured malt whiskies (see page 109) are made in the Islands, notably at Talisker and Ledaig in Skye and at Laphroaig and other distilleries in Islay.

OATMEAL POTATOES

1 lb (½ kg) potatoes, peeled
1 oz (30 g) butter
1 egg yolk
2 beaten eggs, seasoned with
    salt and pepper

6 oz (170 g) medium-ground
    oatmeal
Fat or oil for frying

Boil the potatoes for about 20 minutes, drain and dry well. Add the butter and egg yolk and make a smooth purée. Allow it to cool, then shape into croquettes between a couple of spoons. Dredge in the beaten egg and oatmeal, leave for some 20 minutes, then fry golden in hot oil or fat.

LOBSTER HEBRIDEAN

Fresh lobsters from the Hebrides are of the best.

2 lobsters of about 1½ lb
  (¾ kg)
1 oz (30 g) unsalted butter
1 liqueur glass Drambuie
4 fl oz (120 ml) double cream
For the cheese sauce:
2 oz (60 g) butter
2 oz (60 g) flour
2 oz (60 g) grated Cheddar
  cheese

4 large mushrooms,
  cooked
1 oz (30 g) grated Parmesan
  cheese

½ pint (3 dl) milk
Salt and pepper

Halve the lobsters lengthwise. Remove the meat from the half shells and claws and reserve.

Make a cheese sauce by melting the butter in a small saucepan, adding the flour and cheese and then the milk, stirring well throughout. Season to taste and boil for a few minutes until the sauce thickens.

Now melt the butter in a frying pan and toss the lobster meat for a few minutes. Add the Drambuie and cream, and bind the mixture with the cheese sauce. Spoon into the four half shells, decorate with the cooked mushrooms, sprinkle with Parmesan cheese and lightly brown under the grill.

OATCAKES

These may, of course, be bought ready-made, but this is a traditional Scots recipe.

8 oz (225 g) medium-ground
  oatmeal
1 tablespoon melted bacon
  fat
½ teaspoon baking soda

Pinch of salt
Approx. 6 tablespoons (100
  ml) lukewarm water

Mix the oatmeal in a basin with the fat, baking soda and salt, adding enough water to make a stiff dough. Dust a pastry board with oatmeal and roll out the dough to ⅛ inch thick. Invert a dinner plate over the rolled-out dough, run around the edge with a pastry cutter, then cut the circle into triangles. Lightly grease a griddle, get it fairly hot and cook on both sides until the edges begin to curl. This will take about 5 minutes; stop before the oatcakes brown. Crisp for a further 5 minutes in a hot oven.

ORKNEY AND SHETLAND

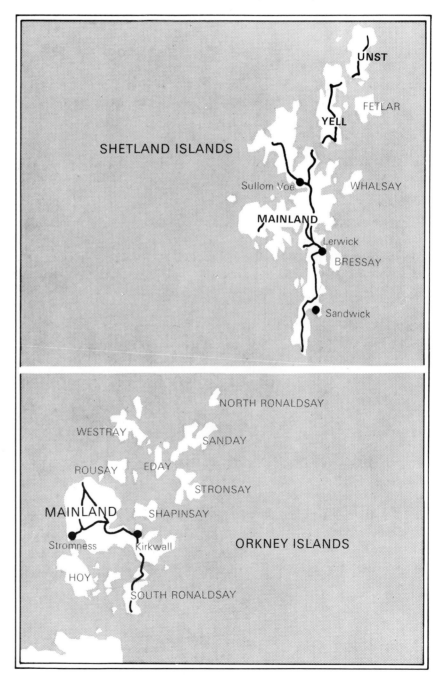

Orkney and Shetland are often mentioned in the same breath as the Ultima Thule of the British Isles; in fact, the southernmost of the Orkneys is only eight miles north of John o'Groats, while the Shetlands lie sixty miles further to the north across a sea amongst the roughest in the world during winter. Most of the larger and inhabited Orkney islands are low lying and occupied in raising cattle, while Shetland (from the Norse 'Hjalt-land' or 'High Land') is mainly upland moor or peat bog, broken by hundreds of tiny lochs. One of its most typical sights are the black and brown sheep and hardy Shetland ponies. Traditionally, the Shetlanders have been known as fishermen who farmed, and the men from Orkney as farmers who fished.

Nevertheless, Orkney and Shetland possess many things in common: the winding inlets or voes — the sea is never more than a few miles away; stretches of barren cliff, battered by the sea in Shetland into tortuous arches and defiles; an almost total absence of trees; the pearly summer twilight, which briefly divides sunset from dawn; and a pervading Norse influence, manifested in place names, folk lore and historical remains.

The 'Watch Stone' at Stenness in Orkney.

The ferry at berth in Stromness.

Both groups of islands were inhabited by an unknown Stone Age people, who, especially in Orkney, have left the most extensive prehistoric remains in Britain. Colonized by the Picts at about the time of Christ, they were visited by early Christian missionaries and from the seventh century were under constant attack from the Vikings. In A.D. 875 the islands were annexed by Harold Haarfagr and were thereafter ruled by the Norse Earls of Orkney until 1468. Thorfinn the Mighty (1020–64) ruled both the Hebrides and a large part of northern Scotland from his hall at the Brough of Birsay in Orkney. His grandson, Magnus, later canonized, was murdered by the co-Earl; and his nephew, the cultured and saintly Rognvald, founded St. Magnus Cathedral in Kirkwall, where both men are buried. From 1230 the Earls were all Scottish; and in 1468 Christian I of Norway, on the marriage of his daughter to James III of Scotland, made over the lands in lieu of dowry. Of the stewards who later administered them on behalf of the Crown, the most colourful were the autocratic and tyrannical Earl Robert and his son Earl Patrick, deposed and executed in 1615, when Orkney and Shetland were integrated with the rest of Scotland.

There are flights to Orkney from Wick, Aberdeen, Edinburgh and Glasgow; the car ferry from Scrabster, near Thurso, skirts the Island of Hoy, affording good views of its towering cliffs and of the 450-foot high pillar of the Old Man of Hoy, before putting in at Stromness on the largest island, Mainland. The only place of any size apart from the capital, Kirkwall, it was once a base for whalers and the ships of the Hudson Bay Company and is a small town of great character, with a single narrow street paved with flagstones running its length and giving access to the old houses and small jetties which crowd the waterfront. The massive and comfortable hotel is grandiloquently Victorian and a twin of that at Kirkwall. Some eight miles away on the east coast, Kirkwall also has a busy harbour and a stone-paved main street, thronged with shoppers, but unexpectedly shared with cars, which appear without warning around its sudden bends and corners.

The town is dominated by the Norman cathedral of St. Magnus, founded in 1137 and much restored during 1912—20. The overall impression is one of robust solidity; an interesting feature is the series of tombstones dating from 1300 onwards, the earliest being Norse in character and carved with a macabre skull, bones and hourglass. The Bishop's Palace nearby is little more than a shell; and much more attractive is the Earl's Palace opposite, built for the notorious Earl Patrick by forced labour during 1600—7. Described as the most accomplished piece of Renaissance architecture left in Scotland, it overlooks a pleasant green, whose trees are among the few of any size in Orkney.

A typical Norse-inspired tombstone, with hourglass, bones and skull.

The most impressive of the prehistoric sites may all be seen by making a circuit of the northern part of Mainland. Take the A965 from Kirkwall towards Stromness. To the north of the road about a mile beyond Finstown stands Maeshow, a huge Stone Age cairn; the burial chamber has been re-roofed and is artificially lit. A few hundred yards away, the four remaining Standing Stones of Stenness, radio-carbon dated to about 2300 B.C., are part of a once-large circle; and nearby stands the gaunt finger of the solitary 18-foot high 'Watch Stone'. A right turn on to the B9055 will take you across the causeway dividing the Lochs of Stenness and Harray to the Ring of Brogar, a great circle of stones in bleak heathland, surrounded by an overgrown ditch hacked out of the rock, of which twenty-seven out of the original sixty or so are still standing.

The northward continuation of the road, the B9056, touches the west coast at the Bay of Skaill, where the well-preserved Stone Age village of Skara Brae is one of the most remarkable survivals in Europe. It seems that the village was hastily evacuated during a sandstorm, and it lay hidden until it was uncovered by another storm in 1850. It has been carefully excavated and numbers some ten dry-stone houses with arching roofs and low entrances, arranged around a paved court with covered connecting passages. They contain stone beds, cupboards and shellfish tanks; and the small museum on the site house fragments of beads, pottery and tools, abandoned by their owners when they left in panic some 4000 years ago.

The Stone Age village of Skara Brae in Orkney, showing a bed in the foreground and compartments in the wall for storing food.

Further along the coastal road, at the north west tip of the island and near the ruins of Earl Robert's sixteenth-century palace, the remains of Earl Thorfinn's hall and of other Norse buildings occupy the Brough of Birsay. The islet is accessible by a causeway at low tide; at other times there is a good view of the old Norse capital from the shore opposite.

After rounding the north coast of Mainland the A966 passes close to Gurness Broch (see also page 140) on the windswept Aiker Ness opposite the Isle of Rousay. The Iron Age tower, still 10 feet high and the best preserved in Orkney, lies at the end of a footpath about a mile from the road. From here the A966 rejoins the main road from Kirkwall to Stromness at Finstown.

Below: The midnight sun over the Brent 'B' platform, some 120 miles off Shetland.

Right: Fair Isle, a remote crofting community and bird sanctuary between Orkney and Shetland.

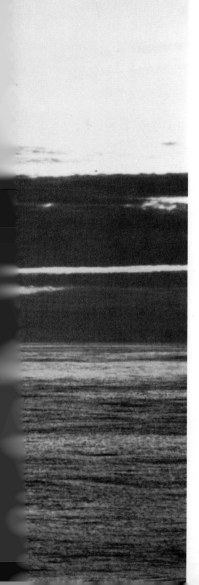

South of Kirkwall, the Scapa Flow, ringed by Mainland to the north and the islands of Burray, South Ronaldsay, Flotta and Hoy to the south, is the famous naval anchorage. It was here that the German Grand Fleet was scuppered after the end of the First World War. In spite of efforts to seal off the Scapa Flow by causeways, booms and block ships — some of which may still be seen as if stranded only yesterday — it was penetrated by German submarines during both wars; and in Kirkwall Cathedral there is a memorial plaque commemorating the 833 men lost when H.M.S. *Royal Oak* was torpedoed in 1939. Flotta has now been developed as a tank farm and terminal for North Sea oil.

The North Islands of Orkney, which also possess some interesting prehistoric remains, may be reached by local ferry services from Kirkwall or by flights from the nearby airport.

To visit Shetland one may go either by overnight car ferry from Aberdeen to Lerwick or by plane from Aberdeen, Wick or Kirkwall. There are now major oil installations at Sandwick in the south of the largest island, Mainland, and in the north at Sullom Voe. Industrial development has been carefully planned, but Shetland's emergence as Europe's largest oil centre is, of course, bound to have repercussions on traditional ways of life. Lerwick, for all its remoteness, has been accustomed to foreign visitations from the time of the Vikings onwards, and its harbour is a frequent port of call for Russian and Scandinavian trawlers. The shops in its flagged Commercial Street behind the waterfront sell the famous Shetland knitwear at very reasonable prices; and in January Lerwick celebrates the 'Up Helly Aa', a torchlight procession culminating in the burning of a 30-foot replica of a Norse galley.

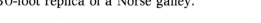

Shetland, of great interest to ornithologists and bird-watchers, is not as rich in archaeological sites as Orkney, but one at least deserves a visit, the 45-foot high broch at Mousa, on an islet off the coast near Sandwick and the best preserved of the five hundred scattered around the north of Scotland. The brochs were built during the Iron Age, though some were still in use at the time of the Norse raids. The typical broch is a hollow round tower about 40 feet in diameter at the base and tapering upwards, with double walls containing galleries and a staircase. It seems likely that they were built as the dwelling places of chiefs, but used by the rest of the community in times of danger.

Half way between Orkney and Shetland is the lonely Fair Isle, purchased in 1948 by the National Trust for Scotland, both to establish a bird sanctuary and observatory and to safeguard its small crofting community. In 1588 the Spanish galleon *El Gran Grifón* was wrecked on its shores, and it is sometimes thought that the intricate patterns of the Fair Isle woollens were inspired by its survivors. Simple accommodation can be arranged at the Bird Observatory Hostel.

Orkney is well known for its cheeses, made in firm rounds. Those with most flavour and bite are from the farms themselves, and one of the best sources of supply is Scott's Fish Shop in Kirkwall, suppliers by Royal Warrant to Queen Elizabeth the Queen Mother. Beyond this, Scott's is world famous for its smoked salmon and Kirkwall kippers. Much of the salmon is smoked for private customers, who send it from all over Scotland, and it is first cured in rum and Demarara sugar according to a secret family recipe. Owing to the scarcity of Scottish salmon, Mr. Scott now obtains some of the fish from Canada — but in both cases the results are outstanding.

As might be expected, the lamb in Orkney and Shetland is excellent.

SALT HERRING APPETIZER
A recipe from the Scottish Tourist Board's *A Taste of Scotland* recipe book.

2 salt herring	1 hard-boiled egg, finely
1 medium-sized apple, peeled	chopped
cored and finely chopped	Lemon juice
1 medium-sized onion,	Salt and pepper
finely chopped	

Soak the fish overnight in cold water. Skin and bone it next day and wash well in running water. Mince coarsely with the other ingredients, adding lemon juice, salt and pepper to taste. Serve on toast.

The mail boat leaving Fair Isle.

140

SCOTS BROTH

Soups made from fresh vegetables feature on most Scottish menus, and they rarely disappoint. Dr. Johnson first tasted Scots broth in Edinburgh, and in answer to Boswell's enquiry, 'You never ate it before?' replied without hesitation: 'No Sir, but I don't care how soon I eat it again.'

1 lb ($\frac{1}{2}$ kg) neck of mutton or boiling beef, in 1 piece

3 pint (18 dl) water

2 oz (60 g) pearl barley, soaked for 1 hour in warm water

2 oz (60 g) dried peas, soaked

Salt and pepper

Chopped parsley

Use in addition a selection of the following vegetables in season to make 1 lb ($\frac{1}{2}$ kg) in all:

Diced celery

Diced potatoes

Diced turnip

Diced carrot

Shredded cabbage

Chopped leeks

Finely chopped onion

Ask the butcher to give you a knuckle bone and put it into a large pan with the meat and water. Bring to the boil and skim. Now add the barley and peas and simmer gently for 1–1$\frac{1}{2}$ hours, depending on the type of meat. Add the other vegetables and simmer for a further hour. Remove bones, take out the meat and dice. Return it to the soup, season to taste and sprinkle with parsley. The meat is sometimes served separately.

CLAPSHOT

A traditional vegetable dish from Orkney.

$\frac{3}{4}$ lb (350 g) potatoes

$\frac{3}{4}$ lb (350 g) turnips

2 oz (60 g) butter

Salt and pepper

1 heaped teaspoon chives or shallots, finely chopped

Peel and cut up the potatoes, then boil them for 20 minutes with a little salt and pepper. Boil the turnips separately for 20 minutes or a little longer. Mash the vegetables separately with butter, then mix together and beat in the chopped chives or shallots until creamy. Serve piping hot.

Index

Picture Acknowledgements

Reproduced by kind permission of Regimental Headquarters, The Cameronians
(Scottish Rifles): **100** top. From *The Clans, Septs and Regiments of The Scottish
Highlands* by Frank Adam, Johnston & Bacon Publishers (Edinburgh and London)
7th ed., 1965: **97**. Reproduced with the approval of the Colonel of the Regiment,
The Gordon Highlanders: **96** bottom. William Grant & Co. Ltd: **109** bottom,
110 top. Susan Griggs Agency: **109** top. Justerini & Brooks Ltd: **114**. Macmillan
London Ltd: **99**. National Trust for Scotland: **48**, **51** top/bottom, **55** bottom, **71**,
79, **95** top, **96** top, **102**, **105**, **116** bottom, **139**, **140–1**. From *Our Railways* by
John Pendleton, 1894: **28–9**. Popperfoto: **101**, **104**. Jan Read: **16**, **17** top, **27**, **33**,
36, **38**, **46** bottom, **49**, **52**, **53** left (top/bottom) and right, **54**, **55** top, **64**, **80–1**,
86, **87**, **88**, **90–1**, **92**, **93** bottom, **106–7**, **111** bottom, **115**, **116** top, **120**, **122**
top, **126–7**, **134**, **135**, **136**, **137**. Royal and Ancient Golf Club: **58** top/bottom,
58–9, **60** top. Royal Commission on Ancient and Historical Monuments in Scotland:
111 top. Scottish National Gallery: **24** top, **98**. Scottish National Portrait Gallery: **9**,
95 bottom. Scottish Tourist Board: title page, **17** bottom, **18**, **19**, **20** top, **21**,
22–3, **23** top/bottom, **24** bottom, **24–5**, **25**, **26** top/bottom, **28**, **30**, **31**, **39**, **41**,
42–3, **43**, **44**, **46** top, **46–7**, **57**, **60** bottom, **62**, **64–5**, **67**, **69**, **70**, **72**, **73**, **74**, **75**
left and right, **76** top/bottom, **78**, **82**, **89** bottom, **90**, **93** top, **94**, **100** bottom,
102–3, **108**, **118**, **119**, **121** top/bottom, **124**, **125**, **126**, **127**, **128**. Shell U.K.
Administrative Services: **138–9**. John Topham Picture Library: **116–17**. U.K.
Atomic Energy Authority: **118–19**. University Library, St. Andrews: **7**, **10**, **11**,
12–13, **20** bottom, **29**, **32**, **37**, **40–1**, **50**, **56** top/bottom, **59**, **61** top/bottom,
77 top/bottom, **89** top, **122** bottom, **129**, **130–1**.